FOREVER FAMILY

OUR ADVENTURES IN ADOPTING OLDER CHILDREN

Ruth Piepenbrink

OUR SUNDAY VISITOR, INC.
Huntington, Indiana

Scriptural quotations used in this book are taken from the Holy
Bible, Revised Standard Version, and from the King James Version.

Fictitious names have been provided for persons in this book other
than members of the Piepenbrink family.

Copyright © 1981 by Our Sunday Visitor, Inc.
Huntington, Indiana 46750
All rights reserved

Design by Thomas Casaletto

International Standard Book No. 0-87973-807-3
Library of Congress Catalog Card No. 81-80894

Printed in the United States of America

For Pip, who makes it all possible

Contents

Acknowledgments

I want to ackowledge, with loving thanks, my family's contribution to this book. Pip insisted I had the ability to write our story when I wasn't at all sure myself. Andy, David, and Lee have done their utmost to stand silently by the typewriter till their mother reached the end of the sentence. Bob coached me in the particulars of preparing a manuscript. Sharon and Jerry, our wonderful children-in-law, nudged me, individually, to remove the completed manuscript from the bottom desk drawer and submit it to a publisher.

Most of all, Ann, Joe, Sherry, Chris, and Eve must understand the depth of my appreciation for allowing their stories to be told as they happened, in the hope that other children might find Their Own Families. It was Christine Acheson Marshall, among us as friend, who dubbed us "the forever family." Finally, I would like to acknowledge, with my gratitude, the concern evidenced for the Waiting Children by the staff of Our Sunday Visitor, Inc.

— R. P.

Author's Note

Fifteen years ago, I would never have thought I could write an encouraging word on the subject of adoption. For six years my husband and I met discouragement and frustration in the form of rudeness, indifference, and borderline abuse at the hands of welfare department employees and superintendents at Children's Homes. Having bared our souls in our desperate longing for another child to raise with our "biological" child, we were teased with the possibility of being allowed to adopt this child and that child, only to have our hearts broken as, time and again, another door was closed to us. In those days, adoption agencies strongly favored the idea of placing children with couples who were unable to have children of their own. Today, I am happy to report, adoption officials are much more concerned with the prospective parents' willingness and ability to provide a real home for a waiting child.

— R. P.

1/10/95 3:13am

Your student, Ashley R
in mathematics for appr
Ashley's progress as of

Ashley is enrolled in
From an initial placeme

Ask, and it will be given you;
seek, and you will find;
knock, and it will be opened to you.
— Matthew 7:7

Ann and Joe

"You have Dad, and Dad has you. I don't have anybody!" Bob meant it as an explanation, and I understood that, but it hit me as an accusation.

He was as near perfect a son as a couple could have: good natured, profoundly intelligent, possessed of a warm and loving disposition. There was no way in which he had failed us in the nine years since he had been born to us. Yet Pip and I had failed him in a way that encompassed every moment of his living and being: we had not provided him with the brother and sister of his dreams.

We were concerned only briefly when the sister or brother we had planned for his second or perhaps third birthday was not born to us. We would adopt him a sibling. From the day following Bob's third birthday, we had been searching. With every passing month and year, it became ever more necessary that we find Bob's sister or brother if the new addition were to be of a companionable age. Our interest in an infant, any infant, diminished as he grew older.

The repeated suggestion of social workers that we could not love an adopted child as we loved the child born of our union only infuriated us. Every child was a gift of God; the manner in which a child would come to us was not significant. Three times we felt we had done everything humanly possible, approached every agency and institution, endured all the insult and heartbreak a couple could. And three times our congenial youngster, who never pushed for his own way in any other matter, looked at us with sadness in his deep, blue eyes and exclaimed: "I want a sister! I want a brother! Mom, you have Dad. Dad, you have Mom. I don't have anybody!" In our own eyes, and in our own hearts, we stood accused.

Once again we renewed our search. There had been an important change in our lives: Pip's job had taken us to a different city, where we found ourselves, miraculously, dealing with welfare department employees who treated us with courtesy and consideration. On a glorious June morning, we met with a caseworker in one of the tacky, temporary offices just then housing the welfare department. Plaster was falling from the ceiling, and cardboard patched a hole in the wall, yet the Taj Mahal could not have seemed as grand to us, for we heard the caseworker say: "I've got a couple of kids who need a home. The girl is seven, the boy is four. They're good, bright kids, not disturbed — so far as we can tell. They just *will* be if we don't get them settled in the right home. Do you think you'd be interested?"

Would we be interested! All that remained was to make the arrangements. At that time the adoption authorities were concerned with a child's appearance somehow matching up with the rest of the family. Well, our family included people heavy and thin and dark and fair and little and big, so we could hardly miss.

Big and broad-shouldered, Pip looks the part of

the football player he's been. Because he's always immaculately attired in a business suit, you have to imagine the football gear. It isn't hard. Over six feet tall, Pip carries his 225 pounds well. My fair coloring is much the same as Pip's, except that my eyes are green, while his are an unusually deep, clear blue. His hair, like mine, is medium brown, the difference being that his curls have only to be combed through, while mine have to be manufactured. Pip's rugged features befit both his size and the strength of his character. My own features are small, appropriate for me. Those members of my family who do not call me Tiny call me Squirt. They'd often teased Pip and me about the Mutt-and-Jeff difference in our sizes. His sister is a blue-eyed blonde; mine has dark eyes and almost raven hair. Oh, and let me not forget my redheaded grandmother and all my redheaded cousins! If a child were to be offered us, we felt sure we could argue a family resemblance somewhere.

The children, it turned out, were blue-eyed blonds, a matching sister-and-brother pair for blue-eyed Bob, whose hair was just deepening into brown from the blond of his early years.

The caseworker filled us in on a little of their background. Half orphaned, the children had lived sometimes with their young and immature mother. More often, they had been passed around from unit to unit of the extended family, sometimes moving several times in a week. When it had become obvious that there was no one in the family to make a permanent home for these youngsters, appropriate court action was taken to make them available for adoptive placement. Our caseworker was as pleased as we were that the ages, sexes, and coloring of the children blended ideally with Bob's to make a perfect family unit.

Her idea of the next step was to set up a place where we could see the children without their knowing that they were being observed by prospective parents. This suggestion came as a surprise to us, and we declined. We were only concerned that the children were legally wards of the county so that there would be no possibility of our losing them on some technicality later on. We didn't care what the children looked like or how they behaved. The social worker then suggested what we know now to be the usual second option. "Take the children for a little vacation," she urged. "They're used to going from family to family. We'll tell them you're people who like children and want to have them visit for a while." We said no to that as well. We wanted the children. We wanted them forever and forever. We knew there would be stormy times ahead while we were learning to know and love each other and live together as a family. We felt sure we could get through those choppy waters better with everyone knowing from the first moment on that we were a forever-and-ever family.

Unused to this line of resistance, Miss Monroe fumbled through her files, apologizing that she had no picture at all of Joe and not a very good one of Ann. She produced a snapshot of a wistful little blonde, her hair askew. We scarcely glanced at it, expressing again our wish for the children regardless of looks or behavior. Having dispensed with the preliminaries, Miss Monroe said she could bring the children on Friday morning. This was Wednesday morning. Forty-eight hours! Six and a half years of wishing, praying, searching, pleading, waiting; and now a scarce forty-eight hours to get ready!

That momentous Friday came at last. It was really, truly happening. The children we had hoped and prayed and scrapped for were to be ours forever and ever. And Pip was taking a whole day off, not a half day or a long lunch hour, to welcome them. As manager of a retail tire store, Pip never took a day off for anything! He did take the vacations he was entitled to, but never ever did he deem it necessary to be away otherwise. Even a day out of town to a company meeting meant, for Pip, making up the time missed on his job itself by working the evening before and after.

That's the way Pip is, always demanding the very best of himself. Ten years earlier, when Pip was managing a smaller store and giving just as much of himself, I had gleefully anticipated that Bob's birth would force Pip to close up shop for half a day at least. But when it came to it, baby Bob put in one of the quickest appearances our doctor had ever known for a first birth — *after* working hours! In part, I think, by way of recompense for that time, and because he wanted the children to understand how very important they were to him, Pip took the whole day off. At that time, Ann and Joe had nothing against which to measure the great event. Years later they would boast, "Dad took the whole day off the day we came!"

It was early afternoon when Miss Monroe drove up and stopped in front of our house. We could see two blond heads bouncing around in her car. Pip, Bob, Pal (our collie), and I all hurried out the door to meet them at the curb. We had anticipated this moment for at least six years, preparing ourselves in every way, and now we did not know how to play our roles. *We* knew that these children were to be ours forever, that we were a family, complete and at last. The children, however, had been told that they were coming for a visit, to spend a vacation with us at the lake! Miss Monroe had warned us that morning by telephone that the children had been misinformed and advised us to let them think they were only vacationing with us. We reluctantly agreed. By now we had been frustrated so many times in so many ways that, at this moment of victorious togetherness, one more frustration was only that. Although we were thrown off stride, we were not downcast.

We invited Miss Monroe and the children in, and they came, the children carrying their clothes in boxes. Our little girl was so thin that I was concerned for her health. Her forehead was a mass of wrinkles, and her eyes had a haunted, hunted look. Our new little boy, though not husky, appeared to be in ruddy good health. He wore a bright smile, and his eyes sparkled. We showed the children their rooms first (the new arrangement was the result of two days' furious rearranging), then all of the house and yard. They were nervous and eager. After a round of soft drinks, Bob took them on a tour of the neighborhood. While Bob was introducing the children to our friends, Pip and I talked with Miss Monroe about them and signed the agreement placing them officially in our home "for adoptive purposes."

Miss Monroe stayed quite a while. She knew better than I the path that lay ahead and was sympathetic about the larger loads of laundry I would be doing, as well as grocery shopping and cooking for unknown tastes. Finally, the tug of other things to do called Miss Monroe away, and though she observed that the children were settling in well, it was difficult for her to go. It is a happy time in the routine of the social worker when a child is placed in a home, far happier than many of her duties. Eventually, however, she said her good-byes, telling the children she would be seeing them again, as we knew she would be.

The afternoon went quickly enough as we helped the new arrivals unpack their boxes. The children had come with good wishes from the world they left behind, for I could see as I unfolded their things, many of them new, that they were far more costly than those we would be buying as replacements when the time came. Despite costly garments, their possessions were pathetically inadequate: there was not a toy, book, memento, or little treasure of any sort.

We had decided ahead of time that we would not deluge the children with toys or gifts. My mother had sent us three little handmade stuffed clowns, one for each child. And Bob gave two of his own cast-iron banks as gifts to his new brother and sister, one shaped liked a kitten for Ann, and a rocket bank for Joe. Aside from their clowns and banks, Bob had an abundance of toys the new children could have, and there was a large sandbox in the yard. We also began the new children's allowances on that very day so that they might begin to learn money management, purchasing for themselves whatever small thing they wanted most.

Our first trip together as a family was to the store late in the afternoon. We bought the children change purses (to contain the new allowances) and toothbrushes, the only things we could see that they would need immediately and did not have. After dinner (a simple, sure-to-please-the-kids affair of hamburger patties, potato chips, corn, and chocolate cake), the neighborhood children got together for a softball game, as was usual on a pleasant summer evening. With a ball bat in her hands, we saw the first happy sparkle in our new little daughter's eyes.

Bedtime that night brought with it a lesson in faith for me. The ball game, as we planned, had run

15

past bedtime. The children settled around while I prepared to read them a Bible story. The bookmark caught my attention by falling on the floor and fairly shouting its message up at me: HAVE FAITH IN GOD. ASK, AND IT SHALL BE GIVEN YOU. Why had I doubted?!

Yes, I should have had faith through the years of searching! Now, I wondered, did we have faith and strength and wisdom enough for the days ahead? The conditions under which the children came dismayed them not at all. They were altogether adaptable to changing environment; we weren't. We had thought ourselves fully prepared, and I suppose we were as able to swim as we could be — without actually getting in the water. We had read every available book on the subject of adopting older children, and we thought we knew most of the answers. It turned out we knew only a very few.

For I, the Lord your God,
hold your right hand;
it is I who say to you,
"Fear not, I will help you."
— Isaiah 41:13

New Rules, New Names, New Happiness

Miss Monroe's car hadn't turned from our street before we discovered that we had been left with children different from any we had known before. It was to be expected, of course. Children who had been neglected would certainly not have been taught the social graces. We had all that to catch up on! Even Ann, whose troubled eyes and worry-wrinkled forehead caused me grave concern, had a way of barking orders at us: "Open the door!" "Get me a drink!" "You have to put a Band-Aid on here!" Commands rang through the house. We reminded each other that only occasionally, and for brief periods of time, had these children been in the care of responsible adults. It must have been great fun for them to have such a hold on a pair of parent-people as to have them hopping up to render these little services.

We were a bit shaken by this turn of events. Still, there were only two new children to three of "us," and we were able to keep up with the demands of the day while still rejoicing that our dreams were really coming true. All heavy sleepers, we slept that first night the sleep of the drugged. It wasn't until the early morning sun shone in my eyes that I realized the house was already alive with the chatter and activity of little children. By the time Pip left for work an hour later, I felt that his leaving me alone with the children was akin to abandoning me!

The children were not disobedient so much as disinterested. They had been, as we knew, here and there and everywhere, often shifting for themselves. We knew all that was behind them and that this was their permanent home. They didn't. They played, romped, cavorted, and injured themselves at an alarming pace throughout the day. By the end of Pip's working day, my strength, Bob's patience, and the family's supply of Band-Aids had all been exhausted. And there were still two weeks till vacation time, when Pip's steadying hand would be available twenty-four hours a day!

We were to learn all sorts of things about our children in the next few days that natural parents — or adoptive parents of infants — learn across a span of years. Ann was quiet, kind (she always had a pet cat in her arms), protective of Joe, and worried (as her eyes and her forehead profoundly emphasized). She seemed to be really happy only when she was participating in an active game. Joe was a charmer. And *mean!* He would constantly have to dash away to kill an insect, the cats ran from him, and Pal had to resort to nipping him in self-defense. No worry wrinkles on his forehead; he wore a bright-eyed smile — *always!* With sad hearts, we observed that this smiling apple-polisher and his worried sister simply didn't cry.

For all his mischievousness, we were as enchanted with our new little son as we were with our lovely daughter. Ann was as beautiful as she was kind. She kept her room incredibly tidy and seemed eager to please us in all respects. I yearned to hold her in my

18

arms and tell her that although we had lost our first seven years, we belonged to each other forever. But I held myself back, unsure of what she was thinking and feeling.

We were apprehensive about taking the children on vacation because they saw no real need for obedience. The nearby lake represented danger as well as opportunity for pleasure. Ann wanted to please us, yet there were so many do's and don'ts to learn. Such things as waving an arm out the car window to catch the breeze were fun to her, but we had to forbid them as highly dangerous. Not only was Joe uninterested in obeying, there were many times when we had the feeling that he was running a series of private test programs to see just how determined we were to have him obey.

Compared to our gladness, our concerns were as nothing. Settling into the cottage, shopping for groceries at the country store — things we had done so many times before — had an added fullness now that we were sharing them with the family of our dreams. Bob had his own brother and sister to play with in the sand, to swim with, and to read to. Sleeping three across in a bed he had once had to himself perhaps symbolized Bob's new way of life — crowded but fun!

You might not think this kind of vacation would be vital for us, of all families. Everything we did all year through, except for the long hours Pip put in on his job, we did together. Neither of us had independent recreational activities. Pip loved football and basketball, and we all went to the games together whenever we could. He and I both loved to travel, and we wandered as far and as often as time and money permitted, always together. Even in volunteer service, we shared our time and interest. All of Pip's volunteer hours, and most of mine, went to the church. Yet, this time away from the pressures of business for Pip, from homemaking for me, with all of us together every minute, was always a time of restoration for us as a loving family unit.

It was all the more so now. When we shopped, we all shopped; when we made beds, we all made beds; when we fished, boated, hiked, or swam, we all fished, boated, hiked, or swam, going from one person's favorite activity to another's, sharing each with all. We think every family could gain from one such week every year; we know it is without fail an enriching time for us — especially in those years we have not felt an especial closeness at the beginning of the week. We invite no guests. The idea is to rediscover one another. We've always come off the better for it. I will always cherish the memory of a quiet row on the lake one evening that summer when Ann said, "I wish we could stay with you forever"; and we were able to tell her that they would.

Joe woke up one morning with both eyes swollen shut. What a sight! Because he was new to us and we did not have his health history, we took him to the doctor's to be sure. (Joe was just then getting the series of "baby" shots he should have had in his infancy.) As would be expected of a resort doctor's office, this one was crowded. The rest of us busied ourselves elsewhere while Pip and Joe waited in his office. While they waited, Pip asked Joe if this had ever happened to him before, when the last time was that he could remember being to a doctor, what that was for, and so on. Joe's responses were limited to "No, Dad," and "I don't remember, Dad." Then Pip glanced up to notice their bizarre question-and-answer routine had attracted several curious observers. More experienced now, when we find ourselves in such a situation, we simply smile at the curious and say: "This is our new little adopted boy. We have ever so many interesting things to learn about one another." Joe's problem turned out to be no more serious than insect bites. At bedtime that night, Pip delighted Joe by fastening a paper sign to his pajamas, warning: BUGS — DO NOT BITE THIS BOY.

By the time we came home from the lake, we had ourselves organized as a family. Ann and Joe were calling us Mom and Dad and had been assured that we were together to stay, a forever-and-ever family. They each had new first names. We had not intended to change the children's names. We thought a name was one thing a child could take from one "world" to the next. The opposite turned out to be the reality. There had been several instances when we felt people were paying special attention to our children after we called their names (and they always seemed to be wandering afield). There is of course always the possibility that someone who knew your child before might recognize that child. At that time the very thought that that might happen terrified us.

Dear friends of ours had adopted two foreign children and Americanized their names by doubling the new name with the old, then gradually dropping the original name. We selected the name Joe fondly, if hastily, one afternoon. Joe was the name of Pip's special friend, and a family name as well. Ann's name had been lovingly chosen almost twenty years earlier when, as a teenage bride, I dreamed of having just such a lovely daughter. I cherished the dream and the name in my heart through all the waiting years. It, too, was not only a favorite name but also a family name. This was a fortunate happenstance. Being a part of the succession of the generations means far more (we realized later) to the adoptive child, appreciative of a loving heritage, than it does to the average natural-born, who takes his or her heritage for granted. Several months later, when the school year had begun, Ann used her turn at the paint easel to draw a large picture of our living room, placing her blonde, blue-eyed self right in the middle. Across the back, in typical second-grade printing, she had scrawled: "I'm glad I'm Ann." So were we!

Before the summer was over, we had a second week's vacation. This time we traveled east to visit my parents. The vacation at the lake was a time of getting acquainted. This second vacation was one of shared adventure. All of our family had encouraged us in our acquisition of the children, and they were as anxious to meet them as we were to show them off. An old and familiar trip, every aspect of it was suddenly new and exciting as we saw it through the eyes of the new children. They were so underexperienced that the simple concepts of *city* and *country* were new to them, and such old-hat things as toll roads, service plazas, suspension bridges, tunnels, and toll booths brought forth awe and exclamations. As we passed from highway to highway and toll booth to toll booth, Joe inquired, "How long till we come to the next payoff?" Our hearts were full of mirth and joy and thankfulness.

Mother and Dad welcomed the children as we had wanted to — as our very own. For now, of course, the children knew the truth. Knowing it and realizing it seemed to be two different stories. It was while we were visiting our doting friends and relatives that the children frequently repeated a request that broke our hearts with each utterance. Whenever they met someone new and enjoyable, which was happening almost daily on this vacation, they would submit a request that went something like this: "Gee, they're nice! When you give us away, will you give us to them?" No amount of assurance and insistence that we were never going to give them away could completely remove their lurking fear that we, too, would pass them along someday. Little wonder, for these were children who had been passed around from week to week, often from day to day, so long as they could remember!

If any of you lacks wisdom,
let him ask God,
who gives to all men generously
. . . and it will be given him.
— James 1:5

Tears, Tantrums, Togetherness

Despite our assurances that they were our children forever and ever, our efforts to make them feel cherished and secure, and the passing of time with them still our children, Ann's worry wrinkles and Joe's brittle smile persisted.

The fact that they did not cry really concerned me. Our caseworker suggested that we perhaps spank them briskly enough for the hurt to trigger the tears the children needed to unloose. I was reluctant to do that. Joe certainly *needed* a good, sound spanking. He disobeyed, pushed always for his own way, disregarded our wishes and instructions, and seemed to feel there was nothing he couldn't get away with if he wore a bright enough smile. It was working for him, even on us, but for different reasons.

Having had sole responsibility for Joe just about all of his life, through even dismal and tragic circumstances, Ann watched over him like a little mother hen. It was to spare Ann any additional worry that Joe went perhaps too long not properly disciplined. Finally the right opportunity came to show her his need for an older, firm though loving mother. Joe jerked away from me as we were leaving the grocery store and

24

dashed out into the traffic. I had him hauled back to safety, upended, and soundly spanked before any of us had time to think about it. As we drove home, Joe — who still hadn't shed a tear — glared at me from a corner of the back seat. I explained to Ann that it had been necessary to spank him. "If Daddy and I didn't love Joe," I said, "we wouldn't care if he were hit by a car." Ann didn't respond; she often didn't. Many times we were left to wonder what thoughts were hidden behind her worried little face.

Joe's first tears came, not as the result of an injury or a spanking, but from a good sound shaking. Ann and Joe both were terrified of the basement. We kept many things we regularly used there. As a family, we were used to running up and down those steps many times a day. Ann would try to find excuses not to go. Joe would go cheerfully to put away a toy or hang up muddy pants. Later we would find the toy or the pants wherever they had landed when he had thrown them from the top of the steps! We wondered what dark memory might have caused this fear of cellars. To offset it, Pip painted our already bright basement a cheery yellow, and we all would go down together as a family and play many games there. Pip said that if the basement was the one place in the house they feared, we must make it the happiest place in the house for them to be. He succeeded. They spent countless happy hours playing there with each other, with cousins, and with neighbor children. It was during one of these otherwise happy playtimes that a crisis occurred involving Joe.

The new playroom was full of children. Deciding he wanted a toy another child was using, Joe simply took it away from her. When I responded to the ensuing bedlam, everyone testified in agreement on the circumstances. Even Joe didn't deny having taken it. "I *want* it!" he shrieked. When I pried it from his hands and returned it to the other child, he protested: "That's not fair! *I want it! I WANT* it!"

While Joe protested my "unfairness," his smile grew broader and broader and brighter and brighter till I thought my own heart would break. That such a little fellow should have been forced to learn to smile and charm the world for his needs and wants! "Don't smile if you're mad, Joe," I said. "When you're mad, you cry!" I shook him as I spoke, and that brittle smile dissolved in a deluge of tears that led to a full-fledged tantrum — a simple, beautiful, blessed tantrum!

I'd had tantrums into my twelfth year of childhood. Tantrums I understood! I carried my wailing, kicking, bawling, screaming little son upstairs to our bedroom, tossed him onto the middle of our double bed, and told him to kick and scream his heart out — just stay on the bed. Kick and scream he did, and it was music to my ears after those weeks without tears.

A regular expert on the subject of tantrums, I let Joe wail and screech and protest until I knew his throat would be sore and his head aching. Then, armed with a damp washcloth, I gathered him up in my arms and rocked him, holding the moist, cooling cloth alternately on the back of his neck and on what I knew would be a throbbing, aching forehead. As I rocked and he quieted from sheer exhaustion, I shared with Joe the happy conviction I had felt during his tantrum. God surely had meant us always for each other. Nowhere in the many pages of the home study compiled by the welfare department did it say that I had had tantrums as a child; yet here I was, fully able to understand the fury this child had felt that could be released only through a tantrum. *My* little boy! Whatever lay ahead for us, from that day on I was absolutely certain that God had intended this child for us. With that certainty comes ever the assurance that He will send us the wisdom and the patience needed to bring Joe to fine manhood.

We were never sure just where we stood with Ann. Seeing that I was going to take Joe in hand, she relinquished her own mothering of him and did indeed often treat him as spitefully as sisters and brothers treat each other in every normal family situation. Yet I could not tell if she approved or disapproved of the way we were handling Joe. Her worry wrinkles began to fade, and when we discovered all of her clothing was a size too large and got her a properly fitting wardrobe, she blossomed into a new prettiness. Still, she seemed distant and not quite happy, timid, with a brooding, underlying sadness, we thought. We wondered often if her heartstrings were with someone in her Other World. While certainly not the provoking child Joe was, she too needed a few spankings along the way; but she didn't get them. She seemed so sad and fearful already that we held back.

Ann's tears eventually found release in pain when she had fallen while learning to ride my big bicycle. Spunky and persistent, she would not quit after minor falls that resulted in scraped knees and scratches. Try she would, and try she did — until she took a really bad, painful fall and the tears came tumbling out.

The weeks went on with Joe happy though naughty and Ann mostly being good yet not seeming happy. One night, the children were in bed, and I was visiting with Pip in his workshop. No matter how long and arduous his day had been, Pip would repair the toys that had been damaged that day, or spend a little time making a surprise of some sort for the children.

We were in the basement, directly under Ann's room. I heard her calling me. To reach her, I had to go to the staircase at the other end of the basement, then upstairs, and retrace my steps the length of the house to her bedroom. I was very, very tired that night, and the effort involved in going to her cost me more energy than I had to spare. When I made it there, Ann calmly and sweetly said, "Good night, Mom." "Good night?" I questioned. "Why did you call me?" Ann replied, "To tell you good night." "You called me up from downstairs to tell me good night when you knew I could hear you from there!?" I forgot her timidity, I forgot her sadness, I turned her over in her bed and I spanked her!

Next morning, Ann came to breakfast singing. She laughed. She made jokes. She was the brightest ray of sunshine at our table that morning. Oh, how we had goofed again! She knew we loved Joe well enough to spank him when he needed it. Now she knew we loved her too. Pip said it in a nutshell: "We've been neglecting that child!"

We knew from our "research" that the children would need to have household jobs to do so that they would be contributing to the care of their own home. I planned these carefully to allow myself a time alone with each child each day, a time when each boy or girl could be sure of my undivided attention. The jobs were selected and geared to fill the needs of the children, not the household. It didn't take long for me to observe that there was more housework, cooking, laundry, and general mothering to do on some days than I could get done. On many of those very days, the children didn't quite seem to know what to do

28

with themselves. I was bouncing around in my mind just how to correct some of the inequities when Bob announced at the dinner table one evening that he had something he wanted to say to Pip.

Having gained our full attention, Bob went on. He had come to the realization that the children of the family now constituted a majority. He and Ann and Joe had decided, therefore, that their opinion outweighed that of the adults and, whatever we thought of it, that they should have a raise in their allowances! Pip pondered this only a moment, then flabbergasted me by agreeing. Fortunately, I was prepared. I had been thinking about which of the little daily needfuls could be ably done by which child, and before they could respond to Pip's compliance, I interjected, "Greater allowances carry with them larger responsibilities," and assigned several additional household tasks to each child. Then Pip added, "I suppose you'll want to know how much the raise in your allowance is? You'll each get one cent more." That odd penny remained a part of their allowances across the years, a reminder that, whatever the numbers, the parents are nonetheless the parents. It was their first and last attempt at mob rule.

Draw near to God
and he will draw near to you.
— James 4:8

Structure, Siblings, and School

With the first regular day of school came the first hours that I had been without the company of and the responsibility for the children in those several months. I confess (with some shame) to a feeling of elation. The summer had been bedlam.

For many years I had prayerfully sought the gift of Organizational Ability, and it had been denied me; never had its absence been so clearly evident as through this summer of enlarged responsibilities and constant interruptions. It was also never more clearly evident what a wonderful husband mine is. While I saw to it that the routine of the household kept going, and taught the children everything from Bible stories to baking an apple pie, it was Pip who seemed always to make life fun. The neighbor children distressed Ann by telling her that the big blue bike she was striving diligently to learn to ride was really not hers, it was mine. It had been mine, true. But I had assured Ann that it was now her bike. Pip had a different approach. He drew her up a title, a certificate of ownership, which she flashed with pride. It was typical of his being able to think from inside the kids' hearts and minds, a blessing to us all, then and now.

Pip accepted clutter and disorder, never needed a button sewed on or one thing that would add to the demands on my time (I would catch him doing for himself the little things I had always done before). He was ever patient with me, and awesomely wise and loving with the children. I had known he was one of the Good Guys before ever I married him, and I loved him all across the years, but never with such a deep sense of appreciation as I did throughout that first summer. Our children had not only brought with them the gift of themselves, they also caused us to find a still deepening love for each other — a real bonus.

At the same time that all this love was stirring about our house, it was bringing home to us as well a new awareness of the wondrous goodness and perpetual presence of our loving Heavenly Father. I went to Him that summer with petty problems and major ones, and never ever did He withhold the guidance or the balm we needed — except, of course, for Organization. I had pretty well given up on that, accepting my lack of it as the Apostle Paul had his thorn in the flesh.

While Organization eluded me, we did develop a sort of routine, from which we broke with a great deal of regularity. By washing twice a week, five changes of clothes were sufficient to see us through. With several growing children, we wanted to buy what they needed but not an excess. Grocery shopping also had to be a twice-a-week activity because our faithful, old but *small* refrigerator, happily, lived on and on. We discovered that the larger the load the children carried in keeping up our home, the happier they were (within the scope of childish attention spans and abilities, of course). Each youngster soon had morning, evening, and weekly responsibilities. The first time one youngster attempted to dust the piano while another was practicing on it, it became noisily evident that a bit of scheduling was mandatory. That first summer we at least determined what *ought* to be done at a given time, and that's about as much as can be said for our success in organizing.

Many of our concerns were for Bob, for whom life surely was not what it had been before. Pip very wisely began taking Bob alone with him to football games, while the younger, earlier-to-bed children stayed home with me. Joe was such a get-insky brother that Bob no longer had a corner of his life to call his own. Ann was in many respects the "brother" he had had in mind, for she loved him devotedly and would play quiet games with him, go shopping with him, and take his side on almost any issue. After the first crisis times that came with being invaded by a little brother, however, Bob developed a real brotherly affection for Joe. It mystified me, for though they were about as opposite as two boys could be, they were devoted to each other. Joe would try scampish tricks Bob would never have considered, yet Bob would make excuses to me for him, even when Bob had been the injured party. Joe returned the affection.

There came a time when Joe had had it with us. He went wailing to Bob, "We can't stand it here anymore! Every time we do what we're not supposed to do, we get punished. You've got to find us kids another place to live!" Having a forever-and-ever family had its drawbacks, Joe thought, but this new big brother of his was a keeper! We had to tell Joe that he didn't have the option of running away. We were a family, and families stayed together and made do. He stayed.

Bob's teacher was marvelous as school opened that year, exclaiming over his new brother and sister. She chuckled with delight later in the school year as she confided (concerning Bob's siblings) that he had told her: "the novelty has worn off!" Of course it does, and it had; but it's then you know that you are a family. There are those who wonder about children accepting each other in a put-together family of our kind. "They are perfect brothers and sisters," Pip assures them. "They pick on each other and fight with each other and are mean to each other just like all brothers and sisters are!" And adoptive parents are frustrated, at times, as all parents are.

It had been so delightful for us to have a long summer of sharing places and experiences with the new children. Ann's teacher had the children draw a picture of something they had done that summer. As Ann was telling me, I imagined her drawing a picture of the Capitol of the United States, a ride in a friend's high-powered speedboat, discovering wild flowers in the woods, the glamour of West Point or Annapolis. Her drawing was, instead, of the night at the lake when the mosquitoes were so bitey we couldn't take a boat ride!

That year I was to learn just how often a teacher could request a conference. Although Joe's kindergarten teacher was experienced, she had never experienced anything quite like Joe. I could not be a great deal of help to her. Had I any simple solution for keeping Joe from being the center of a small disaster area, I would have applied it at home. I thought that as the year progressed and Joe drew needed security from the afternoon hours he and I shared alone together, he would outgrow the need to demand so much attention, both at home and at school. He didn't. By early November, I was used to being summoned on about a once-in-ten-days average by the kindergarten teacher.

On one of these visits, Ann's second-grade teacher stopped me in the hall. She had gone as long as she could without telling me about Ann's behavior. *Ann's behavior?* I wondered. Ann was an angel; a quiet, even withdrawn, sometimes unresponsive angel — but an angel, nonetheless. And she was doing excellent schoolwork. She was also, her teacher advised me, pulling chairs out from under the other children, pushing them out of line — literally pushing them down if need be — to be first at the drinking fountain. Her aggressiveness spilled over on the school playground as well. I could scarcely believe what I was hearing, and when it got through to me, I was very sad indeed: our dear little girl was using company manners at home! She wasn't going to take any chance on losing the first permanent home she'd known. Her experience was that schools took you as you were, families didn't. Her dad, as always, came up with a delightful solution. After telling her how much we loved her *just as she was*, he told her to wear her "good hat" at school and her "mean hat" at home. Our quiet, good one turned into a twinkle-eyed meanie, happily signing herself "Mean Ann" to any message of impishness she could concoct!

Christmas, Caring, and Court

One of the happiest firsts was Christmastime. It had been usual for us to spend in the neighborhood of twenty dollars on Bob, courtesy of Santa. Now we did as we had been doing ever since the children came; we simply divided that dollar amount three ways. It did cost more on a day-to-day basis to be a family of five, despite tax benefits, than it had to be a family of three. Yet in many ways the same money sufficed for us all. Instead of going to two movies in a given period of time, we would go to one movie and spend the other evening having a family basketball game in the school yard or a snowball fight in our own yard. Homemade entertainment was fully as much fun for all of us as the ready-made variety.

When the children came, I had resigned from den mothering and from my several church offices and committees so that I might give all of my time and attention to molding us into a family. All my time and attention had often not been enough, but now, at Christmastime, I was getting a little bit used to our size. We were settling in, starting to know what to expect of each other. With no away-from-home commitments, there was a happy ease about the Christmas season. I found time to polish the neglected wooden floors and even to write personal notes on Christmas cards.

Each batch of Christmas cookies was a new adventure for the children who would be sharing their first Christmas with us. Bob, as did Pip and I, found a deep and rich happiness in explaining the meaning and history of every house decoration and tree ornament. After the church service on Christmas Eve, while we were trimming the tree, I caught the reflection of Ann's happy face smiling from a shiny Christmas ball. Her worry wrinkles were gone at last! My heart was flooded with peace and joy and thankfulness. A part of that, a special part for the parent who has adopted a waiting child, is the joy that this child's gladness comes from being yours. The extraordinary happiness of living out the ordinary traditions of Christmastide totally escapes these children until they come into your world. Small wonder that many adoptive parents of waiting children soon find there is room for one more. It's a happy Christmas tree that is adorned by children who lived in loneliness and perhaps even in want only a year before. It wasn't often that we thought of the children in the light that they had benefited, for we had wanted them very much and were selfishly thankful to have them for our own. But at this time of Christmas, I did think about the difference for them, too, and was thankful for us all.

The children were still not legally adopted that first Christmastime; in fact it was almost until the next Christmas when we were able to go to court for that final step. We asked from the start when we could begin adoption proceedings, for we knew this would add to the feeling of security for Ann and Joe, and we were certainly going to keep them forever, however long and difficult our break-in period might be. Besides, we thought, pestering the welfare department for permission to proceed would help them to understand that we were not turning back and that we were grateful for these kids.

Our caseworker kept putting us off, which might have worried me except for a conversation we had had one day. The routine of large-family living was not an easy one (what with my woeful lack of the Big O), and it seemed that every time she dropped by unexpectedly the vacuum cleaner was out, the ironing board was up, and there were dirty dishes stacked on the counter. She would wave the romping children a cheerful hello, find her way to an easy chair, picking up a pet cat to hold en route, and visit pleasantly, seemingly oblivious of the chaos around her. When I told Miss Monroe on one of these occasions that I appreciated her, she responded — to my surprise — that the department very much appreciated us. They knew these kids were a big undertaking, and they were grateful. I was astounded; it was almost like paying tribute to someone for accepting precious gems, even though those gems required some polishing.

If there were problems, and there's no denying there were, there were also many happy times. In a nutshell, life had become fuller and, in its fullness, richer. Along with remembrances of tantrums and frustrations, there were times of gladness that will always remain etched in our memories. There was the day of the second-grade entertainment, when mothers were invited. Oh, what joy for the parent who adopts the older child, the child who has never known what it is to have the simplest of parental care, and *never* had a parent to share special moments.

Imagine what it's like being the adoptive mother of such a child. Watch the smile blaze across that worried little face when *her mother* actually comes to share with her. Delight in her every stolen glance away from the stage to be sure that you are really there. Be the first one reached when the teacher invites the children to introduce their mothers; be the mother most tenderly clung to — and see if *you* can keep from crying a few happy tears!

Imagine your first Eastertime together. Visualize the silky new dress you've made especially to bring out the color in her eyes. At the moment of apology for the tugging and the pulling needed to comb out tangled curls, imagine the response: "Oh, that's alright," trailing off to a soft and tender, "It's so wonderful to have a mother who cares how you look."

There was the day Joe's baseball know-how failed to match his need in neighborhood play. Bob, never a sports enthusiast, found a book on the essentials of baseball and undertook his responsibility as a Big Brother. Laying the book beside the baseline, where it could be referred to but would not be harmed, Bob demonstrated book-perfect stances and techniques so that his little brother might become altogether proficient in a field not of interest to himself!

Then at last came that day in court. It is not necessary in our state for the children to be present. However, we were so proud of our family that we certainly weren't going to miss this chance to show them off to the judge. Further, we thought the solemn moment of the legal action making the children officially ours was an important time and a memory they had a right to. All of the children attended. They sat on a couch in the judge's chamber while we were sworn in and our attorney asked us pertinent questions. I giggled at the ones, coming back to back, as to whether I was in good health and not employed away from home. I explained to the judge that I saw no way a mother could be either sickly or not in the home and keep up with our three-ring circus. The good judge immediately granted our petition, shook hands with all five of us, and congratulated us on what a fine family we were. We all floated out of the courthouse just a few inches above the sidewalks. Dear, silent Ann, bless her, spoke the words we were all feeling: "This is the happiest day of my life!"

The long hours required of a manager of a retail store seemed even more oppressive after Ann and Joe came to us. Pip had to be at work six days a week, and many times he put in a few evenings as well. Everything we wanted to do had to be crammed into an extremely limited time. By the time we were home from church on Sunday, it was past noon. Whatever outing we planned for the week had to be accomplished in a brief Sunday afternoon. Then another long, hard week with no rest loomed ahead for Pip. Now that we had the family of our dreams, we wanted to fulfill them. Swimming and picnicking were more fun for Bob now that he had a brother and sister with whom to share such outings, and we were determined to find a way to spend more time together. Well, we had asked and we had received. We would, and did, ask now for this blessing.

It was necessary for us to plan as well as to pray, and to consider options, some of which would have necessitated our moving. The very mention of a move of any sort might be distressing to the new children that early in their lives with us, so until there was something concrete, Pip and I decided to keep our plans between ourselves and God. Talking personally and privately was something hard to accomplish now that Ann was part of the family. She had come to us so marked by adults surreptitiously planning a questionable future for her that whenever or wherever we would talk together quietly, we were apt to discover Ann pressed against an adjacent wall, listening. Only now and again would Ann be the subject of a private conversation, and of course we would never have parted with her. Yet how could she really feel sure after her here-to-there past?

In order to have those needful husband-and-wife discussions, we would occasionally suggest that the children play a game together or watch a favorite television show while we "took a walk." Round and round we'd walk, and talk, but always where we could see the house and the children could see us.

After seventeen years with one company, Pip had the daring to change jobs. He was asked to manage a lumber yard in a small town nearby. I was reluctant, for it still required his presence there on Saturday mornings, but he was excited at the prospect. He would have the opportunity to learn the lumber business while managing the retail store that was a part of it. Five and a half days would certainly be better than six had been.

But God was answering our prayers more abundantly than we had thought. After two years, Pip was asked to take a job back in the city. His time in the lumber business had qualified him for a much better position. Pip would be studying blueprints of commercial and industrial projects, estimating costs, calculating possibilities, selling the work, and overseeing its completion. Not only was this work interesting, it used all Pip's skills, from having a real knack with color to overseeing the men. At last he was out of retail, working a five-day week. With no need for a move or disruption to the children's lives in any way, our dream was being fulfilled. Pip had work he truly enjoyed, and weekends belonged to the family. We were able to enjoy many outings, take short trips, and do many of the home projects we'd never had time for before.

One of the first of these projects, a major one, was to build a bedroom for Bob. He had had to share his room with Joe from the moment Joe came. Now Bob is one of those guys who loves to read and rarely tires of his own company, but a private room was a luxury that had not been his since our family had grown. Ours was a large, cheerful, and totally dry basement. We asked Bob if he would like a bedroom of his own down there. Would he! He packed his clothes in a paper bag, gathered up his books, and set himself up in a corner of the basement on a bedroll, encouraging and helping in the months ahead while Pip built his room around him!

*. . . remembering the words
of the Lord Jesus . . .,
"It is more blessed to give
than to receive."*
— Acts 20:35

A Very Merry Christmas

While we were trying to lead the children to an understanding and appreciation of the true values in life, they were helping us to define our own values more clearly. We had slipped somewhat from our earlier good resolutions about keeping from acquiring scads of "things." The children's rooms and the yard and the basement playroom became filled with toys as "bonus days," birthdays, Christmases, and visits from grandparents rolled past. Then came the Christmas when, along with that special item each child wanted and a few surprises and some extras, Pip and I agreed that each of the children really should have a new bicycle. Three new bicycles were not easy to work into our budget, but we managed it — along with all those other things we thought the children might be hoping and wishing for.

We had a wonderful time shopping for just the right new bicycle for each child. It took some money juggling, for we knew that to carry Christmas expenses into the new year dimmed our joy in those coming months and awarded some of Pip's hard-earned income to the money lenders. Among the things we were considering at that time were the contact lenses Pip had wanted for many years. Always, always there was something "more important" to spend his money on; this Christmas was no exception.

The children woke us early that Christmas. We called for them all to stay in their rooms for a few minutes. Pip dragged himself out of bed after three brief hours of sleep, as did I, woolly and weary as always on Christmas morning. Pip went to turn on the tree lights, for this would be the younger children's first glimpse of it. Pip always said that if there weren't another thing for Christmas, the sight of the tree would be enough. This Christmas there *was* everything else. We had the children and each other and hearts full of gladness because we had given them so much.

Bob, Ann, and Joe came out and looked at their gifts more or less methodically without any show of pleasure or even of special interest. It seemed to me they had scarcely glanced at the gleaming bicycles standing together in the corner of the room. Finally Joe asked, "Is that all?" What more he could possibly have expected, I couldn't imagine. "Didn't you see the bicycles?" I asked. Yes he had seen them.

I was tired. I was distressed at what seemed their lack of appreciation. I was disappointed. It must have shown. Bob, Ann, and Joe, too, hastened to assure us that they were delighted with just everything and that their bikes were the greatest. But the moment had happened.

It had been an honest moment. Finally I was honest with myself and fixed the blame where it belonged. Pip and I had taken for ourselves the joy of the Christmas season. We had known the happiness of abundant giving, even sacrificial giving. We had taken the grain of giving, leaving only the chaff of receiving for the children.

As soon as Pip was off to work one morning, the children and I gathered around the table for a conference. I told them that we had made a mistake. Their dad had deprived himself of something he had been wanting for a long time in order to give them things they surely didn't need, perhaps did not even want. Now, with their cooperation, we might be able to even up the score. Along with far too many toys, games, and assorted gifts, the children always received gifts of money at Christmastime. Pip had given me some money as a part of his gift. The children and I gathered together all of our gifts of cash. I searched in the back of dresser drawers for small amounts of money I habitually tucked away there, squirrel-like, against just such a time.

The children were coming alive now with the joy of giving that Pip and I had taken for ourselves the past several months. They hurried to get their savings banks, where they had been putting away something each allowance day. Tapping every cash source available to the four of us, we had about fifty dollars. It was enough of a start, I felt, that Pip would be willing to use family funds for the difference to be fitted at last for the contact lenses he wanted. We made an appointment in his name for a few weeks later, and when we gave to him that card along with the fifty dollars, the happiness shining in each of the children's eyes assured me that this was the best gift they had received this Christmastide.

From that year on, Christmas has been a real joy for each of us. Oh, it's still wild and hectic; we didn't become an organized household, just a family with a satisfying set of values. Christmas cards all too often get mailed *after* the rush; most of the happy things we plan to do invariably get put off till another year. Yet the dreams we dream, the plans we make, the things we do — are happy dreams and plans and accomplishments. The children still wish and ask and receive, but we keep things within the scope of a limited, sensible budget. Like so many blessed American homes today, we have a full share of all the things we need and many of the things we want. There is no way that an abundance of receiving could bring much to us but just that, still greater abundance. And who needs it? even — perhaps especially — a child? when full and plenty is our daily blessing?

As we are not preoccupied with making lists of things we'd like to *have*, we find a great deal more time to think of things we'd like to *give*. Here, too, very little money is involved. Our shopping is done with love and with care. The little children are dependent upon their Christmas savings. The thrifty ones save a little ahead from their spending money as the season approaches; the unmethodical spend *all* of their December allowances on the rest, for they invariably find something special and extra they're certain another will find great joy in receiving. By so doing, they themselves are blessed with the true joys of the Christmas Season, and this is what we would wish for them as well as for ourselves.

Although ours is very definitely a middle-class life-style, it seems to those little ones who have known want and woe that we have wealth without end. Along about July, they start with an occasional hint about what they are going to ask for for Christmas. Generally, that first thing is within the usual scope of expenditure. It isn't until the list begins to grow that we must have a little serious conversation about Christmastime, which the children accept quite well. It doesn't take either age or wisdom to observe that there are more wonderful things to wish for than there is home to hold them. Even youngsters can see that our pleasure comes not in how much we have but rather from our enjoyment of the things we do have. This has led to some serious decision making for the children. Even that is not bad, for we must each make decisions every day of our lives and live with the results.

You may have read somewhere that Santa Claus is believable and enjoyable for children two to five years old. I know I have. We would like you to know that, at our house, *Santa lives*, and he didn't even get started with most of our children till they were past five. Our precious ones who have been robbed of the joys of early childhood cherish the Old Fellow and would provide us with the wool to put over their eyes if need be. Nobody around here pokes a hole in the wonder of it. We know that he *is*, for we know that he was not when he should have been.

Perhaps the very happiest and most meaningful part of our Christmastime comes between the hours of noon and midnight on Christmas Eve. I hesitate to write of it, for we are not to let our right hands know what our left hands are doing. Yet, if friends had not shared their experience with us many years ago, we would have been denied the blessing season after season. At a time when we had been married several years and had not yet been blessed with children, Christmas was lonely — not complete somehow. A coworker said, "Come with us this Christmas Eve if you want to have a happy holiday." He and his wife took us to the poorest section of town, where they left food and toys at the door of a shabby home, shouting "Merry Christmas!" as they hurried away before they could be identified or even thanked.

Our friends had learned that though this family never had much, this Christmas they had no means for any celebration of the Holy Birth. While our friends could not change the family's fortunes, they could and did help them have a happy holiday. Because we had been privileged to have a share in that giving, it was a happy Christmas for us as well.

From that time on, wherever we have been, we have learned from our church or a community agency about some last family, missed by those who would have everyone share in the bounty of the Christmas Season. Then, in those very last hours before the stores close, we hurry in, armed with a list of ages and sexes of children. Our children, with the help of their daddy, pick out appropriate toys. Often the press of time requires one or two of the older children to share the grocery shopping with me at the same hour. By shopping late we get the very best bargains and need never move the groceries from the car before we deliver them. We take the toys home to remove the price tags. Then we add some fancy wrapping paper and tags and ribbons so that parents can wrap the gifts for their children if they want to.

On two Christmas Eves, we have had a sick child among our number, and the sadness is not so much the misery of being sick at holiday time as it is the child's disappointment at not being able to make the trip to deliver bundles stealthily to a home where only the adult has been advised that there would be something on the doorstep. For our children, this is the greatest time of all, since they *know* what such a Christmas surprise would have meant to them.

We are mindful that these families would benefit more from a job or improved legislation of one form or another. But we have never had a job to offer, and we do our best to be informed and involved and do our share in making needful social and economic changes. Yet there are always those who cannot or have not found a better way; and even where the adults might not be considered "worthy," the children dare not be forgotten. While there is ever so much we cannot do, this much we can do. We recommend it heartily for all who would have a very merry Christmas.

In all your ways acknowledge him,
and he will make straight your paths.
— Proverbs 3:6

Woefully Waiting

About two years after Ann and Joe came, I began to
realize that I was greeting Pip at the end of his working day with such bright bits of conversation as: "I did
the wash today. Seven loads." Or: "The ironing board
cover is getting a little tacky." Talk about tacky! Then
I knew that it was about time to rejoin the community. I could scarcely serve my family well with so little
going in my world that I could not even make interesting conversation. By then we were quite used to being
a family of five. We had our daily routines and our
weekly routines. Our house was once again in order.

I discovered then that even Bible School, a teaching assignment I had enjoyed every year until the children came, took more time and more effort when
there were four of us to get off to church every morning, but I loved being involved with people again.

Later I served as PTA treasurer, room mother at
school, and den mother for Joe's Scout group when he
was old enough. One of the boys in the den, a delightful if superactive youngster, was a foster child.
My heart went out to Jody, for he was a little older
than our Joe and still searching for his family!

I had accidentally learned that he was a foster

49

child when he had given me the family name and his "mother" stressed that theirs was not his name. I almost hated her, so eager was this youngster for his own family and so indifferent was she to the concerns of his heart. Jody told me then that he would be going to a different family. He said that his new home would be with a couple where the man was retired and would have lots of time to be with him. Jody knocked at our door early one morning soon after and, with that all-too-familiar brittle smile, told me how he was going that day to where everything would be perfect! He left my heart aching and my mind awhirl.

Each of our children had his or her own bedroom now. We were fully used to ourselves as a family of five. If there were children in the community who needed homes, we surely could add another to our family. It couldn't be Jody, I realized, for he was so close to Joe's age and Joe was barely settled in. Then too, the fact of his placement in a home in our neighborhood would preclude his returning with yet another identity. But if Jody needed a family so much that authorities would place him with a couple of retirement age, then there must be other children in our town who also needed a permanent home. I was haunted for weeks that spun together into months by the memory of Jody's brittle smile. I could not summon the courage to tell Pip what I was thinking. He had gone so far out on a limb to assume the responsibility for a larger family than the one "nature" had given him; he had ever so patiently loved us through the settling-in years; and now I was thinking of asking him to start all over again! I could not get the courage to broach the subject to him. Nor could I get the thought of a child possibly needing a home such as ours out of my mind. So, as always, I took it to the Lord in prayer.

On a lovely day in June, it "happened" that we were seated at the Cub Scout picnic exactly opposite a delightful family who had at least twice as many children as we had. They were a pleasure. Afterward, as Pip and I walked in the park and I was able to get out the perhaps-one-more plea, he said: "I've been thinking about it for months. I didn't know how to mention it to you!"

We waited only long enough to discuss the possibility of a new brother or sister with the children. Ann was thrilled about the possibility of being on the reception committee this time. Joe added his Amen. Bob was satisfied with the brother and sister he had but said he had to agree if a child needed a home. I called the caseworker who had placed Ann and Joe with us, only to be rocked back on my heels. "You already *have* a lovely family!" she said. No denying it. She slammed the door smartly on fingers that had only begun to recover from the sting of closed doors.

Now we didn't know what to do or think. We turned to God for further direction (our faith was growing) and waited none too patiently for His instructions. Several months later, I attended a meeting of the women's organization at our church. The speaker was another caseworker from the very department through which we had obtained our children. She spoke of the woes of the children in her care and, eventually, even of the need for good adoptive homes for those who must be removed from existing circumstances. I trembled with excitement, furious to think that red tape like this might be separating us from our child. I was, in fact, so unsure of my ability to control my emotions that I asked a friend, also an adoptive mother through this department, to ask questions in my stead. My friend confirmed the fact that this caseworker did place several school-age children each year for adoption.

When the meeting was over and many of the women had dispersed, I was able to collect myself enough to discuss our interest in adopting personally with the speaker, Mrs. White. An altogether gracious woman, she explained that, regrettably, one worker might know only of children needing placement, while another worker would know only of seeking parents. What needless sadness was caused by that simple lack of communication!

It was this Mrs. White who was the caseworker for "my" Jody. I was thankful to learn from her that he had been placed in what seemed to be a workable adoptive situation. Beginning the very next morning (after she had had a chance to review our case history), Mrs. White would frequently call to chat with me about the plight of this child or that. I realized I was being interviewed — in an altogether pleasant way.

Mrs. White told me that there were children in her charge who were living with parents who did not want them, were not seeing to their needs, and sometimes treated them brutally. Yet, even though she could testify that these children were suffering gross neglect, some of them exposed to grave danger, the judges would often refuse to remove them from their "natural" families. There were not enough adoptive homes available for school-age children, and the judges would risk hazard to a child in most instances rather than see him or her grow up in an institution. Judges, much to the child's detriment, often seem to feel that any home, no matter how unsatisfactory, is better than Children's Home.

I talked with Mrs. White at length about abusive,

neglectful parents, a topic I had pursued years earlier with Miss Monroe. It was clear to both of us that going through the biological procedure of bearing a child does not of itself make a person a loving parent, any more than saying the words of the marriage service makes one a loving wife or husband. The love has to be there. The sad common denominator among almost all biological parents of abused and neglected children is that they themselves were abused or neglected, and not all of them were, by any means, on the ragtag edges of society. Unless a man or a woman has grown up in a loving parent-child relationship, he or she has no reservoir of happy experience to draw upon and pass along.

Over the next few months, there were occasional telephone calls from Mrs. White and discussions about those children who were her concerns, always boys. This fact suited us fine. Although adopting a boy would give us three boys to just one girl, the bedroom arrangement was suitable for the addition of either, and we really didn't care.

Unlike the first time around, when I had abruptly resigned from community responsibilities with the coming of the children, those things in which I was involved were coming to natural conclusions. Our home routine was very much in hand, and I was curiously without away-from-home responsibilities. I was then asked to take an office in our church that would be demanding and time-consuming. I had no intention of accepting the post, for we were eagerly expecting another child, and who could tell how much time and attention that child would need? Explaining this to myself one day, I sounded to my own ears distressingly like those people who seem to make up the bulk of all church and school groups, the I'd-love-to-but people.

The only honest excuse I had was that I might have an excuse later. I talked it over with Pip, and he concurred: the work of the church had to go on. Not much use raising children if we didn't do our share to keep those things going that could make it a better world for them to live in. If a child did come to us, perhaps even a terribly troubled child, there would be time enough then to reevaluate the situation and resign if necessary. On Tuesday I accepted the office; on Friday I attended a training meeting. En route to the meeting, one of the women asked me if we had heard anything concerning our adoption application. I told her there was nothing definite yet but that we had learned from experience that when these things happened, they happened fast.

By dinnertime that evening, Sherry was our little girl, living in our home, eating with us as one of our family.

This was one of several times when I have had cause to reflect on the exactness with which God moves about the checkers of our lives. Had Sherry come to us three days earlier, I would not have taken the office. There was a real joy in feeling God had wanted me to accept this responsibility in His church. It caused me to do my very best and, whenever either home or church commitments threatened to overwhelm me, to lean ever more heavily upon Him for instructions. He never let me down. The combination of these responsibilities resulted, as it turned out, in great fulfillment and satisfaction in the months ahead.

Take delight in the Lord,
and he will give you
the desires of your heart.
— Psalm 37:4

Sherry

A telephone call early in the afternoon alerted me that
Mrs. White was going into court and, after conferring
with the judge, might have one of the boys she had
discussed as awaiting placement. I called Pip to
share this information. He always let his office know
where he would be when he was out making calls;
with these developments pending, he would keep in
even closer touch. It happened that the high-school
students had the afternoon off, and Bob was home to
steady me in my excitement and help me give the
house a little special going over against the possibility
of the caseworker or even our new little one coming.
To emphasize our earnestness and our confidence, we
arranged the chairs around the table for six.

The other children had arrived home from school
when at last the phone rang. Casually, slowly, Mrs.
White drawled, "Wasn't there one of the women in
your church group who said she wanted a little girl?"
Nobody specifically said she wanted a child except
me, I remembered. And who said we *didn't* want a
girl, I wondered? A girl would be just fine! "Do you
have a girl?" I asked. "Do you have clear title to a
girl?" Well, yes, except for one tiny, routine detail,

she did. "How old?" I asked. "Six," she answered. At that time, Joe, the youngest of our children, was ten; we would have taken a child up to nine. Six, however, was just fine. Mrs. White said she was a nice little girl. Except for the fact that she was woefully fat, the child had no special problem. She was a first grader, Mrs. White informed me. She thought she would make us a good child. "Let me call Pip for his approval," I said, "then I'll call you right back."

I have to laugh at the people who think adoption is less meaningful than the biological method of acquiring a child. Each brings with it indescribable peaks of anguish and ecstasy. I hung up hastily and could not for the life of me direct my mind as to how to call Pip. No number would come to my mind. Turning quickly to search in the directory for the familiar number, I could not bring to mind the name of my husband's employer! Telephone still in hand, I turned to the children and pleaded, "Where does your father work?!" They quickly supplied the name that so ridiculously escaped me. Still I had to search for the number.

Pip's office, not surprised that I was seeking him, told me at once where I could expect to find him. I channeled through the switchboard of a large company to the office of the buyer where Pip was making a sales call. A little girl suited him fine. I was only to ask if we could start her in our elementary school under our name on Monday morning. Excited himself now, Pip said he would get home just as quickly as he could. I called Mrs. White once again, who said she had to go and get our little one. If it were agreeable, she would bring her directly here. She was anxious to be on her way, for it was almost usual for this little girl to find no one at home after school and not even be able to get into the building. She would wander off, looking for someplace to go, and might be hard to locate. On this day and forevermore, she would have someplace to go!

Now that the commitment was made, the waiting began. We realized that we hardly knew a thing about this child. We did know she was a girl, and that's an edge we had on people who walk the corridors outside a delivery room. We didn't know if she was a blue-eyed blonde, like the other children, or a black-eyed brunette. I entertained the thought that the strain of red hair that keeps cropping up in our family might pop up again! It crossed my mind that she might not be Caucasian. All of us were — so far — but adoptive families can and do cross racial lines these days, and I couldn't remember ever having discussed the child's race with Mrs. White. What an exciting time! We didn't even know what kind of a car Mrs. White drove, so every time any car approached, we all ran to the door. Happily, one of those cars turned out to be Pip's. All of us were together then to greet our new little girl when she would arrive. We paced back and forth in our excitement. Another edge — or handicap — that the adoptive parents of an older child have is that we know we will remember the first sight of each other forever. A dozen times, I went to the mirror, checked my skirt and blouse, and touched up my hair. *Do I look like I'd make an alright mother?* I wondered.

I shouldn't have concerned myself. When at last Mrs. White pulled into our drive with a little honey-brown head showing through the car window, we all ran out to offer our welcomes. As I opened the door on our little girl's side, Mrs. White said, "This is Sherry." And Sherry, clutching her cardboard box of meager

57

earthly possessions, scowled at us all, lowered her eyes to the ground, and walked to the house without ever looking up while we flitted around, exclaiming over her beauty and expressing our welcome. Sherry was dressed only in a sleeveless dress, panties, shoes that were splitting from her fatness, and a jacket. She wore neither socks (she owned none) nor slip. For wintertime in our northern clime, her clothing was certainly inadequate. No wonder she had been sick so often. Within her memory, we were to learn, she had had pneumonia three times.

At our urging, Sherry sat down — on the very edge of the couch — her hands clutching each other, her beautiful brown eyes staring down at her hands and at nothing else. I perched on the arm of the couch, as close as I felt I dared get without intruding. Mrs. White, Pip, and the other children arranged themselves comfortably around the room, and we endeavored to make small talk. Mrs. White was delighted with Ann, who had been almost exactly Sherry's age when she had come to us. Her six years with us had changed her from a worried little old person to a lovely, radiant youngster. Mrs. White, we knew, was seeing a before-and-after and rejoicing in it.

Sherry did have huge dark eyes instead of the blue eyes now predominant in our family. Those brown eyes were exactly like those of my sister and my mother. I commented on that fact for Sherry's benefit, and for Mrs. White's, for she had placed this child with us hastily, knowing that this youngster needed a home immediately and that we were eager to have another child. The happenstance of her family likeness was a happy extra. Neither compliments nor small talk, however, could bring Sherry out of her glaring silence. Mrs. White had a cup of coffee but, though it was now well into mealtime, declined to join us for our evening meal. We had a dinner of leftovers gotten together during floor-pacing time. We had reached the point of being able to keep household routine functioning under any circumstances!

Concluding that Sherry wasn't going to respond, Mrs. White said her good-byes. Pip followed her to her car to learn if Sherry had any special fears and what parts of town we should avoid so as not to stir up unpleasant memories. At the same time, I took Sherry by the hand. She did come agreeably enough with me to the kitchen while I checked on dinner and got ready to serve it. Sherry had still not spoken a word, and I knew the sooner we got her to talk the better it would be. Of course, I knew that she was in first grade, but rather than give her a chance simply to nod a reply (I was an experienced person with troubled children by now), I asked, "What grade are you in, Sherry?" "Readiness!" was her reply; her first word announced a problem. Ours was one of the schools in the system that did not have a class in reading readiness. Just then Pip came back in the house, and he and the other children began romping and wrestling together while I put dinner on the table. Sherry could only hold herself as an outsider for moments. Before I called them to sit down, she too was tumbling and wrestling.

We kept our eyes carefully averted during the meal so as not to notice her table manners — or lack of them. Sherry was not yet happy, but she was conversational, for which we were thankful. So many times across the years, it had been difficult to impossible for Ann to give voice to her feelings. We hoped our new little one would be spared this distress. As we were finishing our dinner, Sherry exclaimed,

"That's the first whole dinner I ever had!" Knowing that children will say almost anything under these circumstances, I discounted about 50 percent of it, but I was intrigued enough to pass her comment along to Mrs. White when she called in the morning. "Well," Mrs. White answered, "I *know* she's lived on fudge bars and pop for the last three months!" In the bitterly cold wintertime!

As soon as dinner was over, we telephoned all of our relatives long distance and spoke in glowing terms of our new little daughter. She said her first hellos to them all. Then, still with a sense of urgency, we bundled up and began our trek around town to visit nearby relatives and close friends. The little girl who didn't have a place to get in out of the weather at 3:30 in the afternoon was the belle of the ball throughout the evening for half a dozen doting families. We made no effort to cut the evening short because of things we had learned from the other children's experiences. Ann had been sad and sleepless at bedtime when first she had come to us, complaining often of stomach pain. ("An attention-getting device," the good doctor declared, thereby introducing a phrase that was to be used frequently in our household: "It is bedtime that is painful.") Joe was often openly belligerent at bedtime, and that, too, was worth sidestepping. By the time we did come home again that first night, it was long past the bedtime hour, and Sherry was too exhausted to wonder about her new life or the old one. She was asleep, nestled against Ann, almost before she was in the bed.

At the crack of dawn, the house again bustled with activity. We had to rearrange the bunks from Joe's room, since he would remain a single, to Ann and Sherry's. One of the early morning sounds was a call from Mrs. White to see how we were doing. We had a good laugh together, for after only twelve hours of Sherry since she resumed talking, we understood Mrs. White's grave concern for her when she was silent! A quiet child she surely wasn't.

We moved through the day at a fast clip so that Sherry would have no time to feel lost. We were at the stores, shopping for a coat and shoes and underthings, almost as soon as they opened. We would have purchased dresses as well, except that Sherry was so fat it was impossible. It took more than a little shopping to find a boxy all-weather coat that looked nice and would keep our big little girl sheltered from the weather. After returning home for lunch, Pip worked with the older children to get the room exchange finished. I took Sherry to the fabric shop, and together we shopped for patterns and material. It was interesting to me that Sherry had no concept of someone's actually making a garment. She was amazed to realize that we could take cloth and an envelope of paper pieces and actually *make* a dress. She was to stand for hours in the coming days and weeks, watching while this "miracle" occurred and reoccurred.

Because of her special figure problem, the patterns that would suit her just then were limited. I purchased a basic A-line style that I could vary half a dozen ways with ease. As is our custom in teaching the children always to make their own decisions and live with the results, I encouraged Sherry to choose fabrics she liked. She chose one with gaudy, three-inch stripes, splashed with five-inch daisies! Hardly a pattern to minimize her size. We purchased it, however, for I had promised her her choice. We used it for her robe — to be worn in the privacy of family living. The other fabrics were chosen by her from a selection of three or four suitable pieces I had preselected. Mother's learning must go on and on too, it seemed.

The clerk at the fabric shop overheard me asking Sherry what her favorite colors were and kept watching us with strange sidewise glances. Rather than have her think I had just kidnapped Sherry, I told her that this was our new little forever-and-ever girl and that we had a lot of catching up to do. "Isn't she a treasure?" I boasted, and the clerk and a few interested customers as well had to agree that she was. The wandering little girl of twenty-four hours ago was now the star of this brief drama. Nor was her reign in the center of things to end, for I sewed well into the night to complete a pretty and flattering Sunday dress to be worn to church in the morning along with her new coat and shoes (and a little furry white hat dug from the ever-providing "useables" box we kept in the corner of the basement).

We went into church early and sat down as much as usual as we could, considering our pride and happiness, with Sherry tucked between Pip and me in the pew. Then, noticing one person and another who had added their prayers to ours in our search for Sherry, we took her around to introduce her. Other friends stopped by at our pew before and after the service. It was a happy hour for us all. In the afternoon, we traveled out of town to visit friends in other communities lest the busy whirl suffer a letdown too soon. And that night I once again began making a dress at bedtime so that Sherry would have something suitable to wear for the next day.

*All things work together for good
to them that love God.*
— Romans 8:28

Sherry Shares the Shambles

Sherry's chattiness was not only a delight to us; it was a window to the Other World. Gradually, we came to regard Sherry as an ambassadress from the land of children in need. The very nature of their neglect and/or abuse in their early months and years deprives many of the ability to communicate with those of our society who want to help.

Ann, a gentle, loving child, was, by her seventh year, bereft of tears. Under the slightest pressure, she became unable to speak. Joe was more typical. He found voice to demand his wants but not to explain his reasons. But Sherry was different. With her ability and, apparently, her need to verbalize, she was a fountain of revelations for us, almost from the very start.

It is my blessing or my curse that I can push myself physically only so far. Working into the small hours night after night while staying on the go all day finally caught up with me in the form of a heavy cold. I have always been able to pace myself by taking little catnaps, dozing in an easy chair for ten or fifteen minutes. The children were used to my need for naps, and they knew I roused instantly if they needed or wanted me, or if they got into anything they shouldn't. So, after these several days of being on the go night and day, a fresh cold slowed me down to my usual routine (Sherry had enough dresses to last for a little while by now). After school one day, I curled up in Pip's great easy chair and dozed for a few minutes. When I opened my eyes, Sherry was standing as close against me as she could without actually climbing onto the chair or into my lap. I was surprised to find her that way, but I gave her a hug and a love. Seemingly satisfied and happy, she went off to play.

The next day the incident repeated itself. This time it occurred to me to assure Sherry that I was perfectly alright, that I usually rested a little late in the afternoon before I prepared dinner. "My other mother slept all the time!" she volunteered. "We couldn't ever get her awake! She never got up!" Of course and alas! I should have known better. Sherry's other mother, a young and beautiful woman, was deserted by her husband shortly before the birth of her fifth child. Her parents, who lived nearby, thinking she should have managed her life better and not gotten in such a predicament, let her and her children figure the best way out of it they could. The woman's immediate escape was alcohol. Then drugs. Once aware of the plight of the children (someone must notify the authorities when there are children in trouble!), social agencies moved in with a barrage of aid, ranging from immediate financial help to psychiatric analysis, job assistance, even foster-home care for most of the children, while an attempt was made to rehabilitate their mother.

This care and counseling went on over a period of several years, during all of which time Sherry was left with her mother. The idea was that Sherry would provide companionship and encouragement for her mother. During this time, Sherry suffered from a woefully inadequate diet, constant impetigo, three rounds of pneumonia, a tonsillectomy, during which no adult accompanied her or visited her at the hospital, and a sunburn so severe that it left her terrified of sunshine. She also had the sole care of the four younger children when they were occasionally reintroduced into the home in the hope that their mother would begin to care for them. Yet, on the day when disposition was to be made of the case (Sherry was then six years old), the judge implored her mother to keep Sherry. He believed in natural mother-child relationships!

It was incredible that Sherry could have come through those years the happy child she was. Most children would not have, and our institutions today are full of children so badly damaged that many never fully recover. Sherry has such a built-in, look-for-the-bright-side attitude that she was spared the collapse lesser neglect and abuse would have precipitated in most. Within hours of arriving among us, she made us realize what a bunch of squares we had become. She saw beauty in everything: "Boy! Everybody's got neat cars out here!" (We'd been taking them for granted.) "*Look* at them diamonds!" (a crystal chandelier in a friend's home). "Gosh, we have swell lunches here!" (a peanut butter sandwich, an apple, and a cookie; a toasted cheese sandwich and a dish of green Jello; a bowl of soup, a baloney sandwich, and an orange). If ever there was a humbling experience, it was bringing Sherry among us.

There for a while, it was fun times all the way. The thing she loved most was to go; she'd been nowhere and, except for struggling to care for little children, she had done almost nothing. Everything was an adventure, and she couldn't get enough of it. We

65

called her our "go girl" (go-go girls were then in fashion). No matter who was going to back a car out of the drive for the simplest of errands, Sherry was ready to go along. We visited where we could and thought of places to go in an effort to quench her thirst for going. Even going to the grocery store was an adventure for her. Taking her was an experience for me as well. Sherry's vocabulary was approximately that of a sea captain's parrot. She always stayed glued to us in stores, and we would travel down one aisle and up the next with Sherry exclaiming in innocent profanities over the beauty of the light fixtures and informing me as to which brand of beer was superior to another. And me a newly elected church official! Yet how could I but delight in this precious child and give chuckling though reverent thanks that she had been entrusted to us for molding and modification into His ways.

The first week that we had Sherry, we attended a covered-dish supper. Sherry was resplendent in the last of her new dresses, and we were altogether happy and pleased to have her with us. The people in attendance were family groups of our own neighborhood, all interested in children and the community. We thought Sherry to be a wonderful advertisement for all the little lost children in the world yet needing homes, so pretty and vivacious was she. I whispered to Sherry as we approached the food tables that she could take anything she liked but that she must eat whatever she took (a hard-and-fast rule in our family). Sherry took six kinds of potatoes — the food she was familiar with — and nothing else.

Sherry's joy and satisfaction in having a family were obvious. The household ran ever so smoothly throughout her time of coming, and though the initial week, in which I spent long hours sewing, was tiring, there were no real tensions or major problems. It was almost as though we could sit back as observers and watch a family member coming into her own, something we'd been too involved in to savor the first time through. At the close of each meal, Sherry, who sat at my left, would come first to stand beside me. I would put my arm around her and hold her for a few minutes. After that she would move to Pip's end of the table, stand in the circle of his arm for a few minutes more, then skip away happily to join the older children wherever they were.

Sherry had a thing about wanting the child to be, as she put it, "in the middle" of its parents. When we went for a stroll, she would walk between us. In church, she would sit between us. For her, a happy picture invariably featured a young one between its parents, be it a people baby, a lion cub, a song sparrow, or a colt. We even arranged the three wrought-iron fish hanging as wall decorations in our bathroom Daddy-Baby-Mother fashion at Sherry's request. Whatever they may lack in artistic composition is made up in satisfaction to a little girl who wants a pair of caring parents for every creature.

We realized later that Sherry had almost no adjustment problems because ours was a different home to come into than it had been for Ann and Joe. Now the routine of the home was clearly established. Of necessity, a day and a time had been determined for all usual household chores. There was seemingly no question concerning behavior, privilege, responsibility, or discipline for which there was not a ruling already made that needed only to be adhered to. There was nothing that Sherry could think to want, to do, or to try that Joe hadn't before her; and we stood ready to give her our response with calm and ease. *Joe's in-*

*defatigable defiance was largely responsible for forc-
ing our family to achieve the order that enabled it to
grow graciously!*

The children found it was fun to be a foursome.
They played Ping-Pong doubles (atrociously) by the
hour and joined together in other games that were
enhanced by a fourth member.

Ann, like Bob, was a quiet child who enjoyed
long periods of her own company. This time we didn't
wait a few years to consider the possibilities. We simply chalked off another corner of the basement and
went to work.

Fear not, be not dismayed;
for the Lord God . . . is with you.
He will not fail you
or forsake you. . . .
—1 Chronicles 28:20

Siblings for Sale

One of the things Pip had asked Mrs. White the evening she brought Sherry was if she knew of anything Sherry might fear. Mrs. White didn't. Yet, before the end of her first week with us, Sherry's screams woke me in the middle of the night. She had had a nightmare in which someone was trying to take her away from us. The same nightmare was to return often in the weeks and months ahead.

I shared her nightmare, for in Sherry's case, and hers alone, there was a possibility that everything might not be fully settled at that time we got her. There was that "tiny, routine detail," arising like a wraith in the night to haunt us. Sherry had been brought to us at a time of desperation by a loving and conscientious caseworker who took the only way she had of sparing this youngster additional trauma that might never have been reversed — and she had told us that at the time. Sherry's one and only brief visit to the Children's Home had come at a time of terrifying crisis in her other home. While she was there, she had been taunted by the other children because of her weight. To take this child there again, however briefly, could be damaging. So Sherry was brought directly into our home, and now our hearts were entangled in the red tape.

The day the case went to court, the adults of our extended family — all across the nation — joined in fervent prayer that Sherry would never have to return to the terror of her old life. Our relatives joined us in begging God that she should be forever ours. The caseworker who represented Sherry's interests telephoned us the instant she left the courtroom that all was well: Sherry was indeed to be undisturbed and could be ours forever and ever. After I had spoken my thanks to her for letting us know at once, I paused for a larger thank-you to our kind and loving Heavenly Father. I pondered prayerfully over all the other abused, neglected, abandoned children as I returned thanks that our precious one had been spared from a return to the old ways.

There are so many children, rescued at the point of disaster, housed temporarily at an institution or a foster home, only to have to face again neglect, abuse, and despair because someone in authority thinks the "family" or the parent might somehow be saved by sending the child back into an impossible situation. If only the children had a voice that could be heard! Our Churches are concerned about the staggering incidence of juvenile crime, and everyone wonders what should be done. How can we establish effective correctional institutions? they ask. I weep with frustration; our nation is filled with the very institution we need to get the job done — the caring family. Pip has often come home from church meetings, fuming over the money and effort that go into Children's Homes, which are able to help only a relatively few children, when a handful of committed families could do the job at no cost to anyone but themselves.

Well, Sherry moved from that world to this one. No longer does she suffer the terror of ever being returned. Her other fears we came to know gradually, and they were an interesting accumulation. The same little girl who was loath to be confined to a play area consisting of my view from front or back door held to our side with a death grip when we took her shopping. Trying to unbend little fingers enough to allow the blood to circulate through my arm, I learned that Sherry was often taken to a store and "lost" there by her mother, who would slip away and leave. Sherry would then be there, frightened and alone, except perhaps for the younger children in her care, for hours and hours. So badly did these ordeals mark our little girl that after more than a year of being our child, she was still clinging tightly to us in the stores. Again and again, she would point out to us a child — a toddler in a stroller or a baby in a buggy — fearful that that child, too, had been abandoned. We would assure her that this was not the case, but how do you convince a child who has frequently been abandoned that people just do not go away and leave their children in stores? The first time or so we told Sherry that a parent was near at hand and went on about our business. She remained unassured, however, and we learned simply to stand inconspicuously nearby, keeping a watchful eye on the little one until a parent stepped into view and took the child along. Then, and only then, was our little one content to go about our own family's affairs.

Her second novel fear was of houses with an upstairs. It took us some weeks to realize this. A clue was the familiar arm clutching as we passed through an older neighborhood where almost every house had an upstairs. Sherry had lived in one dingy, drab apartment after another in such older homes, and it was in these dwellings that she had so frequently been left alone with smaller siblings to care for, often hungry and cold. No wonder anything that reminded her of those days terrified her. We hadn't realized what a world of ranch houses we lived in. We thought we might mellow this fear by showing her happy times in a similar structure, only to note that all of our friends and relatives were currently living in sprawling ranches!

Another of Sherry's fears became known to us on our first early summer vacation together. She had happily helped to choose a bathing suit for herself, proud that her figure was getting down to a size to look pretty and feel comfortable in one. Sherry hurriedly put on her new suit, as the other children did that first morning at the lake, but then she wouldn't step foot out of the cabin. "I'll get sunburned," she announced. "No, of course you won't," I assured her. "Daddy and I won't let you stay out till you burn. We'll watch and you'll be just fine." I didn't convince her. She stayed in the cabin, though I was certain that she very much wanted to be with the other children playing by the lakeside. So, back to the rocker we went, and Sherry, in yet another narrative of The Times Before, told how her mother had sent her with a neighbor girl to the swimming pool at the city park and left her there from morning till evening for three consecutive days. By then Sherry was so badly burned that she stumbled about the apartment, looking for a place she could fall asleep, she hurt so bad.

Some tears — on both our parts — later, I explained to Sherry that we have to use care in almost everything we do and everything we use. The car is wonderful and takes us all the places we want to go, but Daddy must drive it with care. Nobody loves to eat more than Sherry and I, but we don't completely stop eating to avoid getting sick or fat. We just have to be careful about what and how much we eat. So it should be with the sunshine. I would watch the time and the girl very carefully so that Sherry could play on the beach without fear of burning. Once she was convinced that we knew what we were doing, Sherry trusted us. She got her sun in small, supervised doses and came home with the beginnings of a healthy tan.

Sherry carried another burden: she worried about her little brothers and sisters. She had only been here a short time when she asked at the dinner table one evening: "Afterwhile, are you going to adopt more kids? You'd *love* my sisters and brothers!" Anywhere but the table! I, unfortunately, had food in my mouth and almost choked. It had been such a difficult decision, in every way, to acquire her, and we were absolutely certain we had completed our family. Pip, who recovered first, explained to Sherry that she was our last. He went on — very kindly — to tell her that just as we had searched and waited for her, there were families who had searched and waited and would be thankful to have each of the other children. We knew, and did not pretend otherwise with her, that they would be waiting at the Children's Home till the legal work was completed. I told Sherry that I would ask our caseworker about them and tell her when they had found their own families.

In the meantime, Sherry named her dolls for her siblings. Caring for them, after all, had been her responsibility. Worrying where their next meal would come from was a part of it, as was having clothes presentable for them to wear. Sherry would poke around the kitchen, happily discovering food supplies and commenting about leftovers that would make another meal. It took a few weeks of assurance and fulfillment for Sherry to realize that three meals a day would be forthcoming without her having to plan or prepare them.

Sherry loved being able to take a bath often. She was also concerned about having her clothes mended and ironed. Among her scant array of clothes, were things mended, pathetically, by dear little Sherry herself. She assured me she also cooked and ironed, though we didn't let her do these things for fear of her suffering a burn. Indeed, we were thankful she had escaped being burned when she had had to do them.

While Sherry felt a continuing concern for the little ones, she cared for her dolls, tucking them in, keeping them warm, dressed, fed, and entertained. At last the day came when I could assure Sherry that all her brothers and sisters were settled in permanent adoptive homes. Within the week, the children held a lawn sale of extra toys and Sherry sold her "siblings" at the rate of twenty-five cents apiece. At the age of seven she traded half a dozen years of responsibility as a "single parent" for a dollar's worth of spending money. No wonder she began to sing at her play and work.

There was never any looking back, only gladness that she had escaped. About that time, Sherry announced that she wasn't going to have any kids when she grew up. "They mess up your house!" she stated. Pip and I almost choked on that one, too, for children do mess up your house. We thought we had extended ourselves to include that little one among the messers-up of our house! However, we understood the terrible burden the little children had been to her. While we took a certain guarded delight in her statement, we cautioned the other children never to kid her about it or even mention it. Surely, we felt, the day would come when, having had her chance to be a child, Sherry could anticipate the pleasures of motherhood in its proper time in her life. (And it has.)

The caseworker who had placed Sherry's sisters and brothers and supervised their adoption adjustments felt strongly the need for sibling separation. She echoed our own feelings. We have been ever thankful that it is the policy of our county's welfare department to split up children from the same family when they are made wards of the county and place each individually. We had lived in another county where children were destined to grow up in the Children's Home unless someone appeared to take a group of five or six, as they often come. Of course, this almost never happens, and the children are institutionalized until adulthood. The tragic situations in which many children are born and live their early years is not their "family situation." Their families, truly, are those people who want them and will love them and care for them forevermore. This caseworker, having witnessed the plight of the children and studied widely, insists that older adoptive children must be separated from the siblings with whom they share their dreadful memories. Otherwise, they are reminded again and again of scenes and situations it is needful they forget. That they are willing to make that adjustment and turn from one life to another has been illustrated by each of our adopted children.

While Sherry was settling in, assuming childish responsibilities in our household in place of the huge ones she knew before, she was also slimming down. Two weeks after she came to us, Joe and Sherry burst in from school, he in a righteous rage, she with a few smiley tears enhancing her prettiness. "Those guys called Sherry fatso," Joe announced, "and I beat 'em up!" We had hoped a new little sister would help Joe develop a sense of responsibility. Now if we could keep a bit of peace in the neighborhood. . . . I acknowledged then — and only then — Sherry's "chubbiness." I told her that children didn't understand and would tease. I also told Sherry that although we hadn't mentioned it to her, she was already on her way to being slender. "You are a chubby little girl because you didn't have the opportunity to eat the right foods," I explained to her. "It isn't so much a matter of how much you eat as it is of what you eat. Since you've been our little girl, you've been having foods that will help you to get thinner. One of these days you'll be just as slim as Ann is!"

Oh, but could every mother of a fat child see the radiance of that pretty, round, little face! I told her that the celery she was eating every day as an after-school snack was making her thinner because it had no calories in it. Sherry pronounced celery "sorry," an ironic mispronunciation, for it made her altogether happy — food she could eat while becoming "slimsy." She was interested in learning what the slimsy foods were and often would ask about a dish being passed, "Has them got much cowrees?"

The whole family joined in an intrigue to help Sherry lose weight from the day she arrived. Pip was especially adept at diverting her from her cravings for between-meal snacks. He could be counted on to come up with some amusing distraction for her until the hunger pang subsided. To take the edge off her appetite, I had been giving Sherry a small glass of skim milk about a half hour before mealtimes. If someone were lacking a spoon, we would ask Sherry to

76

get it. If a cat wanted in or out, we would ask Sherry to open the door. She enjoyed her role, and we saw to it that she was never without sufficient time or food. Sherry was kept from eating too much without ever being aware we were at work on her special problem.

I bought the skimmiest of milk and had the older children quietly pour hers from this special source. I bought low-calorie jellies of the same flavors the rest of us were having. I bought water-packed fruits, simply serving Sherry's portion ahead from the low-calorie source. Best of all, I managed not to make an issue of her weight. Her happiest day on her way down to normal size came when Sherry returned to school after spring vacation week. "The teacher could tell!" she called to me as she hurried home from school. "She could see I was gaining weight down!"

Soon Sherry was slim enough to run with ease and jump and even climb trees — happy activities that had been denied to her by her enormous fatness. Best of all, she looked pretty in her clothes, and no one could tease her any longer. Years later, Sherry told us that children of her old neighborhood told her she was so fat she was going to explode. She had lived in fear of that, too.

Because Sherry was settling in so well; because our money was still holding out; because we discovered the room in our hearts was not nearly filled, we reversed our earlier decision and applied for another child. There was just that little matter of finding the courage, once again, to broach the subject to each other.

Your Father knows what you need. . . .
— Matthew 6:8

Dear, Darned Doggy

At this time in our lives, God gave us a good gift — a great black dog. Many years earlier, He had endowed us with a tiger cat who, despite ordinary appearance, was above and beyond the usual pleasureful pet, a special gift of God. While Bob was still an only child, she was his playmate, confidante, and constant companion. She was a welcoming committee for the new children. Beyond that, she had such a sensitivity to human need that her granting special attention to some member of the family was often my first clue that things were not well in the heart and life of someone dear to me. It did not come as a great surprise, then, that God once again chose to bless us with an extraordinary pet, though this great pup seemed at first more a commotion than a blessing.

I hadn't thought to ask for a great black dog. I hadn't thought to ask for a dog at all. We had a dog. We had two pet cats and four children. Had anyone asked me, I would have said that we did not need — and even that we did not want — another dog. Yet, without planning ahead to do so, the children and I stopped to visit friends who had a mother dog and one nondescript black pup. I was surprised to find myself thinking: *That pup will be exactly the dog you need to raise with your children. He will surely be large; he is a large puppy. He is black, and you know you like black dogs. And he will surely be a good dog, and a good, big, black dog would be a wonderful thing to have. Ask for him.*

Well, I put a stop to the foolishness in my head then and there. No one *asks* for a pup. You *accept* a pup. And this one had not been offered. Forthwith, I removed myself from that place to get my thinking straightened out. I never did.

We had a dog, yes, but Pal, already beset with the maladies of old age, could not live much longer. Having two pet cats was an adjustment from three minus two plus one, for in the prior six months two of our beloved cats had died in their old age, and, despite the addition of one new cat from the SPCA, our hearts were lonely. Because our children were — and would be — such special children, most of them having known far more than a child's share of loneliness and want and tragedy, and all of them having had to make such great adjustments, for them the addition of a new dog before the loss of the old seemed suddenly sensible. Grief over losing Pal, when that time must come, could be tempered by the companionship already established with a new pup.

But do be sensible, I thought. *You do not acquire a new pet without discussing it with your husband.* But my husband was away. Besides, I knew what he would have said had he been home. With fear and trembling at my boldness and foolishness and in fervent prayer that my friend's phone would be out of order, that she would not answer, that she would have promised the pup to her own children or someone else's if it was not God's will for us to have him, I dialed her number and asked, "Are you looking for a home for your pup?" "Yes," she said, "if you will take him. I know he will be a member of your family." That was true. We took the puppy home. Pip came home and said all the practical, sensible things husbands who have foolhardy wives need to say. Nothing I didn't already know. But as he spoke all those acknowledged truths, he was gazed at by huge puppy eyes, and nothing sensible mattered. "Brute" stayed.

He was a problem. He was every sort of a problem. He didn't whimper at night in his first loneliness for his mother; he *yelped* all night. He stayed in the yard only until we became confident he would. Then he went everywhere and dared us to catch him. When we tied him, he became hopelessly entangled in the rope. He quickly grew to be huge (as we had hoped he would), the abler to snitch and to chew other people's possessions, and the more catastrophic the difficulty of his belated toilet training. The sensible thing, undoubtedly, would have been to keep him in a confined area out of doors and feed and water him a lifetime through. Yes, the dog would have lost, but oh how much more our family would have lost!

While we were caring for Brute through all these difficult learning days, his heart was growing in love for us, as a pet's heart can and will, given the chance. Big as he was, Brute was afraid to go outside in the dark by himself. One of us would go out with him. We took him almost everywhere we went because the look in his eyes didn't allow us to leave him at home. He got carsick on all but the smoothest, straightest interstate highways. For Brute's sake, we had to plan our outings to those places accessible by such roads. He loved water, so we sought picnic sites by rivers, creeks, and lakes. He sometimes pushed his way out of the car in dangerous places; we are thankful to our dear, good Lord that his puppy ways didn't bring him to an untimely end. While we were trying — in vain, it sometimes seemed — to teach Brute the particulars of coming when called, staying in the yard, and, most urgently, of correct elimination procedures, he was rewarding us with the constant gift of himself. Although this pup was a tremendous care, he provided delightful comic relief in our lives.

The children could depend upon being awakened by the pup stealing away whatever bear or doll they were sleeping with. If they were not easily disturbed, Brute would stand on them, if need be, while grabbing away their toy, provoking the chase he enjoyed. Any new sound or strange sight would cause him to tilt his head to one side, and now a little farther, and still a little more, till you would think his head would come unscrewed. The girl whose job it was to carry up canned goods from the basement shelves taught Brute to carry the cans in his mouth. Brute took pride and pleasure in his "work." He also insisted upon wages. If a biscuit were not forthcoming upon completion of his trek up the stairs, he would not relinquish the can. Brute later learned to carry a basket. Sometimes he used his basket to beg for food. If you should pretend not to notice, he would flip the basket high into the air. When it landed with a crash, it was difficult to ignore. Sometimes Brute would wear the basket on his head as if it were the latest mode in Easter bonnets. Then there is the toss of the head that says more clearly than the spoken word, *This way; follow me!* and leads you to the refrigerator, where more head tossing directs you to open the door for his inspection.

He played football with the children, knocking

them out of the way while he stole the football, if he could, to make the run. He couldn't sit on the sidelines whenever the children tussled. Brute would join in on the side of the underdog (under*child*?), nipping and shoving the other. He would come to the aid of the other child once the balance of power had shifted. Sometimes he would change sides half a dozen times to keep the contest even.

Brute would bury his bones in the large sandbox that had been specially made for our children and their friends. When Brute selected a spot for his treasured bone, mounding up sand above it in a miniature pyramid, all the children respected the area, pretending they couldn't tell it was there. On grocery days, the cats enjoyed sleeping curled up deep within the empty grocery bags that we had put on the floor just so that they might. Brute soon learned that a fifty-pound bag on the floor invariably held a cat. He would run into the room, grab hold of the back of the bag, pick it up high enough to spill out a grumbling cat, never losing so much speed as to fall victim to a slashing paw if the cat chose to take it for more than a good joke. Then there were those few times when Brute got in the shower or tub with one of us. He did love water!

While we wailed and lamented and questioned ourselves for assuming the additional responsibility of caring for a pup, we laughed till our sides ached. This great dog brought love and warmth and untold fun and happiness into our home. It wasn't until a few years later that we were to think upon the fact that he had done a great deal for the children besides bringing them happiness. Because of their love for this delightful pet, the children became more responsible than they ever had been before. I don't mean that they were responsible for feeding him or seeing that he had fresh drinking water; it is not fair to an animal to make him dependent upon a child for his basic needs. But because of his funny, foolish puppiness, this great, strong, young dog had to be constantly protected from himself.

This was never more bravely done than the day our tiniest girl tried to keep the great dog from charging out the front door. Almost failing, she grabbed his tail and hung on, shouting for assistance while being towed belly-whopper style across the threshold and onto the lawn. The dog was saved from his own foolishness, and the girl was even more staunchly and proudly a responsible citizen than before. Even the more irresponsible of the children, we noted, put him on a leash of double strength and walked him along the streets with the least traffic, lest tragedy befall him. The more patient of the children spent hours teaching him to sit and to stay, and praising him for coming. Our fine veterinarian said that if he hadn't learned to come by the time he was a year old, he never would and we would have to confine him for his own safety. It took Brute three years, but learn he did. He learned the limits of our yard, to stay in the car regardless of the temptation to leave, and to come when called under any circumstances. Happily, he outgrew his car sickness. None of this means that the veterinarian was wrong, but simply that love and perseverance can and frequently do belie the "facts" about an animal's (or a person's) limitations.

My grace is sufficient for you,
for my power is made perfect in weakness.
— 2 Corinthians 12:9

Wait, Wonder, and Weep

Once again we had cause to observe with wonder and
thankfulness the loving touch God used as He guided
our lives. On our return from brief business and pleasure trips, our friends and neighbors informed us that
the welfare department had been making their official
inquiries. They were bringing our "home study" up to
date so soon after we had requested another child.
This could mean only one thing: they needed us! We
had worked too often and too closely with the welfare
departments of our own and other counties not to
know that they were always understaffed, underpaid,
and overworked. Taxpaying citizens want and need
their services but are stingy with tax support. The urgent work that must be done today gets done, but
much other important and worthwhile work must be
put off to another day. At this point in our experience
with the department, we knew that to have our home
study brought up to date this promptly meant something.

A few days later, Miss Lyndstrom, our newly assigned caseworker, called to ask if she might visit us.
Inviting her to our home required no special effort on
our part, for unlike the first time a caseworker was to

call and we housecleaned from top to bottom, we knew it would be enough simply to have our home normally clean and orderly, a courtesy we would extend any invited guest.

It was pouring rain the afternoon she came, and after visiting with her for a little while, the children withdrew to the basement playroom while Miss Lyndstrom and I talked privately. Although Pip had feared the welfare department would think we had used all the extra room in the house with the addition of the new pup, she seemed not to notice him at all. In some respects, I was as skittish as a first-timer. Now we knew what a precious addition each child was to our family, and we did already have "a lovely family." I felt a little as though the community had entrusted us with the diamonds and the emeralds and we were asking for the gold as well.

I invited Miss Lyndstrom on a tour of the house, showing her that we now had a full five bedrooms, Sherry's or Joe's available for sharing with a newcomer, and that we had added a half bath since Sherry's coming. I also told her that we had at last accepted the fact that a two-door sedan was no longer suitable for our growing family and had traded it in on an eight-passenger station wagon. I wanted to be very sure she understood that we were ready and able to become a family of seven.

It seems she was convinced, probably before she came. Then Miss Lyndstrom gave me the surprise of my life. "Would you take two?" she asked. "We have a brother and sister who may or may not have to be moved. They have been abandoned twice, and if they must be moved again, it will be very difficult. We need a special home for them, one that we know will be their permanent home where they will not have this happen again." I was flattered, of course, that they had this much confidence in us. I was relieved, too, for obviously a second dog along with four children and two cats did not preclude our acquiring two additional children.

And so we had our up and down moods in the days ahead. It was difficult even to know what we wanted. The children Miss Lyndstrom spoke of were living in a home that had been approved for their adoption, but the marriage was in difficulty. This was very understandable to me. Pip and I had been married a long time, knew each other extremely well, and wanted our children desperately; but as Bob and, later, Ann and Joe came to us, it was a challenge in many ways to the strength of our marriage. We prayed that God's will should be done for the couple and the children involved, and for us and our children. While we waited and yearned and wondered if we should, we continued in this tumultuous springtime to delight in the precious gift of the comical puppy God had blessed us with.

Along with this care in our hearts, we were both carrying tremendous responsibilities — Pip, with his work, and both of us, always, with home, family, and church. Our responsibilities there required formulating plans, recruiting helpers, and, of course, much telephoning and going to meetings. These requirements on our time and energy came precisely as Bob was graduating from high school, with the attendant activities for himself and the family, and while Ann was having her farewell round of junior-high events. Many times I was tempted simply to resign from away-from-home activities to give all of my time to being with, doing for, and enjoying the children. I did learn that "in my weakness, then I am strong," for there was no way I could meet the demands of a day unless I first took a time of quiet prayer for direction and renewal. After that, I observed that the days always fit together somehow.

One morning, six weeks after Miss Lyndstrom's visit to our home, she called to tell me that they would not be needing to move the children after all. I was grief-stricken and thankful at the same time. We were thankful for the sake of the couple, unknown to us, who had saved their marriage and would keep these children. We were grief-stricken for ourselves, for, despite ourselves, we had named them and had begun to think of them as part of our family.

Moments after the call came, I had to leave to attend a Christian women's luncheon. The first person I met was a woman I frequently visited with at these luncheons. When she asked me how I was, I burst into tears and told her the news that had just come to me. She offered to pray with me — right then and there. As other women jostled about on their way to the tables, this lovely woman asked a blessing on those children who were not to be ours and a blessing on the child who, in their stead, was intended for us. Until this time, I would have had an uncomfortable feeling about praying as she did at that luncheon for us and for the children. Yet, from her prayer, I drew the strength I needed. I have always been indebted to her for having the courage of her kindness.

We were able to relegate those children to what-might-have-been, following them with our prayers alone. We resumed a time of waiting, busy as we were and blessed, 'tis true, with a cup already running over.

Now who is there to harm you
if you are zealous for what is right?
— 1 Peter 3:13

Chris

Finally we put pressure on the department to get Chris. I called them up and said: "Look! Either you have a child who would fit into our family or you don't have. We're an approved adoptive home with a bedroom arrangement suitable for the addition of either a boy or a girl up to eight years old. Do you have such a child, or shall we look elsewhere? I'm *certain* there's a child somewhere in the world needing a home, and enough time has been wasted."

When I hung up, I had to laugh at how times had changed. To think that even to dial that number and plead our interest, years before, had made me tremble with fear! Having a lovely family does give you confidence. The Poor Innocent I pounced upon that day said: "Don't go out of the county or to another agency yet. Give me twenty-four hours to see what we can stir up. I'll have Miss Lyndstrom call you." The next morning I had a commitment that required me to be at church for the entire morning. When I got home, Bob said Miss Lyndstrom had called and wanted me to return her call.

You would think the excitement would ebb, that somewhere along the line as the family grew there would come a time when it did not really matter whether or not a new child was to be yours. Not so. We were as tremblingly excited that day as we had been, before Bob was born, with wondering if I were really pregnant; as we had been when Miss Monroe called to say that Ann and Joe would be ours; as we had been while waiting and wondering about Sherry.

I tried again and again to return Miss Lyndstrom's call. Every possible complication that could keep a call from being completed occurred. The welfare department's lines were repeatedly busy. Sometimes their number would not ring at all. On one occasion, when I finally got through, I was cut off before Miss Lyndstrom answered her phone; and when at last I completed a call to her desk, she was gone for the day. At eight o'clock the next morning, after Pip had gone to work and before any of the children were out of bed — the very moment their switchboard would be opening — I was again on the line. This time I reached Miss Lyndstrom immediately. "Mrs. Piepenbrink!" she exclaimed. "I have a possibility! Had I reached you yesterday, I would have had to tell you there was no one, but now there is this possibility. Will you talk to another caseworker?"

The other caseworker shared an office with the woman with whom we had been working and the Poor Innocent I fussed at a few days earlier. She had been looking for a home for a child who met exactly the specifications we had outlined. In fact, she had been looking since *before* we had renewed our application! Mrs. Jentz hit the high spots. Chris was four or five — she'd have to check — had been at the Children's Home for several years, and the county had had wardship for many months. Frankly, she told me, there was such a press of more urgent things to be done, and

89

Chris was safe and cared for and used to being there, that finding a home for him had had to take a back seat to her other duties. Knowing that she would have to make a personal visit to our home before she could place him here, and wanting him right now, that very day — I asked if she could come out that morning. "Not this morning," she said. "I'll come early in the afternoon." "Good! We'll run the vacuum this morning," I responded. Ah, how delightful it was to think of caseworkers as ordinary, understanding people!

I ran down to Ann's room, shook her awake, and said, "You may have a new little brother by nightfall!" Usually a gradual riser, Ann leaped out of bed and hugged me a ribcracker, exclaiming as she did, "Really? That's wonderful!" I never loved her more. Even as we hugged each other, I marveled at the depth of love in this youngster, and at the immense importance she placed on every child having a home. She knew that every new child meant greater demands on our space, money, and time. She truly had not one thing to gain beyond the knowledge that one of the world's homeless children would have a family, yet she found this much joy in being a part of it!

We roused the rest of the children, who were also excited, made an official declaration that we would not attempt to do the laundry under the circumstances (this would have been laundry day), and everyone went to work lightly cleaning and seriously tidying the house and grounds. There was nothing for Pip to do at this point except share our excitement and continue his day's work. Among other things, we added a leaf to the dining room table and pulled the third chair up along the boys' side. Just two days later, we would be taking a pleasant day's journey, and we wanted him to share the experience with us.

Good as her word, Mrs. Jentz came in the early afternoon. Welfare department people are always interested in visiting with the children. As they become better acquainted with them, they can better estimate the prospects for children who might yet be placed with a family. Mrs. Jentz was so interested in all the aspects of their rooms and their lives the children were willing and eager to share with her that I thought we would never get around to that magic time when I would sense the correctness of saying: "All right, children, you are excused. You may play together downstairs while Mrs. Jentz and I visit. Bob, you'll stay with them?" At last it was accomplished.

I think it was more in what Mrs. Jentz didn't say than in what she did say that told me about Chris. She didn't, for instance, tell me that Chris had a communication problem. She did say, "Chris will talk *to me*." I told her of Ann's earlier need to write to us sometimes when speech was impossible for her. She never told me that Chris was belligerent. She did tell me that the older boys at the home, in whose care he had been placed, were inept. I told her about the time Joe wanted to leave us because of our own "mishandling" of him, and how the togetherness of family won out in that and every other circumstance.

After Mrs. Jentz told me that Chris had a sister who had already been placed in an adoptive situation, she began to list *for me* all the reasons necessitating sibling separation under these circumstances. I could have listed those very reasons for her. I interjected that each of our children had biological siblings who had also found Their Own Families; the situation would present no problem in our household. She said then that she felt this was a family in which Chris would fit. "He is a cute-*looking* little boy." Her emphasis left unsaid, I was certain, the kind of *acting* little boy he was!

At last she was down to what she knew was the big hurdle. Chris, she said, had been tested — under adverse circumstances — and was found to be below average mentally, though she found this hard to believe. He could count; he seemed, to her, bright and outgoing, always. However, she felt she had to tell me that his IQ score had already cost Chris one chance for an adoptive home. My immediate response was to say that I wish he had not been tested and that she hadn't told me his score. There is no way a child who has been abused, abandoned, bereft of any loving experience, and totally cut off from the usual everyday experience of early childhood can be tested with even a remote degree of accuracy. But he *had* been tested and he *had* scored poorly and she *had* told me.

I had to tell Pip. Once again I was able to reach him in the middle of his working day, and when I told him Chris was available to us, I had to add: "He tested low. We can't be sure that we will be able to send him to a public school." Without a moment's hesitation, Pip said: "He has to grow up somewhere. He needs a home, doesn't he?" I can assure you, no woman ever loved her husband more than I loved Pip at that moment.

Now that we were at the place where I thought nothing could stand in our way, Mrs. Jentz seemed a bit evasive. It seemed she simply couldn't go and get Chris that afternoon. There were duties to be taken care of in her office that could not be handled by anyone else. "Couldn't *we* go to the Children's Home and get him?" I asked. "Oh, would you?" she said. I've chuckled over that many times in retrospect: we were willing to commit a lifetime to this child, and she was reluctant to "inconvenience" us to make that little trip!

My assurance that we would be delighted to collect our own removed the very last obstacle. Mrs. Jentz called right then, on our telephone, to tell them to expect us. I was standing in the middle of the room (really too excited now to sit still) when the connection was completed and she said, "I've found just the right home for little Chris!" The voice on the other end yelled, "Yippee!" Embarrassed, Mrs. Jentz recovered quickly. "They really like little Chris out there," she said. "They're awfully glad he's found a home." So was I. If he was that much of a corker, he really needed the stability of a solid family situation. I felt a little flattered, too, for I was certain then that the Lord had taken us at our word and was sending a Problem Child our way. We knew that with His guidance we could work through whatever the days would bring.

I had rechecked with Pip about a time for picking up Chris, and he was sure he could break away so that we could be there by five. Mrs. Jentz relayed the information and added, "If I know this family, they'll be there at five." As a matter of fact, we were there at twenty minutes before five.

Before Chris was brought out to us, Pip asked a passing young employee if she would tell us about him. What a predicament to put the poor youngster in, I thought, after the few bits and pieces I had already put together about Chris. Pip was prepared to live dangerously, and there was nothing the young woman could have said that would have caused us to leave without him. Perhaps she sensed this because, after some stalling, she blurted out, "He's pretty ornery sometimes!" I was getting the idea that he was.

A secretary worked up some papers for us to sign that would make Chris officially ours. A few minutes later, a door opened, and a kindly looking, plump, grey-haired lady carrying a cardboard box walked in. She was accompanied by a sturdy, broad-shouldered, handsome little boy. I had forgotten how small even a large-for-his-age just-turned-five was! Before my mind could register that this darling little guy was ours for the taking home, Pip had sprung to his feet and swept him up in his arms in a great bear hug. Then we all came to life and gathered around, spilling out a noisy chorus of greetings for our new one.

His housemother had been standing quietly by the door. As we were ready to go to the car, Chris, without a word of suggestion from anyone, turned back to her and gave her a big bear hug. How much that must have meant to her, I thought then, and how much it told me about the loving heart that apparently was hidden not very deeply under a few behavior problems.

It was time for us all to go home for our first dinnertime together. While I was getting a meal on the table, Pip and the older children began dismantling beds once again, for with the acquisition of a brother, Joe regained possession of the bunk beds. All the while Pip was working, Chris was staying so close to this newly acquired father that Pip would literally tromp on him if he took a step backwards. Just once did Chris come far enough away from Pip to take a second look at me. He brought out one of Joe's toy guns and said, "I've got a gun, Mom." *Mom*, he had called me, and though I was thankful he could and would talk to us, it made me a little sad as well. To accept us so fully and immediately, he must have spent his little lifetime yearning for a family.

That brief conversational line was all I got from or saw of Chris till dinner was on the table. Then, as with each new little one, he assumed the spot closest to my end of the table so that I could see to his servings, cut his meat, and so on. This was really the only time Chris was closer to me than to Pip. He tagged after Pip constantly. When he called him "Dad," you could almost see a golden shine around the word. Inasmuch as it is possible for a parent to be ignored in a usual living-together situation, I was. Happily, Chris was our fifth, and though I loved him from the word *Go*, my satisfaction as a mother did not depend upon his affection. I was only amused and deeply thankful that a little boy who obviously had spent his lifetime yearning for his Very Own Dad should have acquired the world's best.

Without comment, Chris ate everything in sight at dinnertime. They had told us they would feed him before we picked him up, since their usual mealtime was earlier than ours. Chris admitted that he had eaten there, but he ate fully and heartily here as well. We soon learned that Chris never stopped eating as long as there was food in sight. We had to limit his portions to keep him from overeating. We wondered if Chris's eating habits were an unconscious reaction to an infancy in which he was quite literally starved and had suffered rickets because of it.

After dinner we went once again on a quick whirl of visits around town, during which Chris, though speaking very little, complained that his ankle hurt. It appeared that he had bumped one anklebone against the other, and I thought his fussing about it was largely a bid for attention. We put a little soothing cream on it and tucked him into bed. We were pleased to learn that Chris was accustomed to saying a bedtime prayer (earlier he had said grace before his meal). Chris had come from the Children's Home with an appropriate and adequate wardrobe and half a dozen favorite toys, including his teddy bear, two books he enjoyed, and a few personal mementos. His were the best table manners I had ever observed in a five-year-old, and there were no cusswords in his vocabulary. He was a loving and responsive youngster. We felt indebted to the public servants who had so lovingly cared for our child until we found him.

Difficult to Place,
Delightful to Raise

As the next morning dawned bright and beautiful, there was more to do than could reasonably be planned. There was yesterday's laundry (a necessity), today's grocery shopping (another necessity), and preparations for tomorrow's all-day outing. Of course, first things must come first. Though I knew he was fully able to dress himself, I indulged myself and dressed Chris. He enjoyed this bit of mothering, too. Then we went about the house hand in hand, visiting with the big children as they awoke, locating the little table and chairs that had come all the way down the line from Bob's little years. We put them in a corner of Joe's room, along with a bushel basket for toys and a little bookshelf for his personal treasures.

I cut from a calendar two especially peaceful, colorful scenes. One was of a cowboy watching his cattle graze in a golden field at the edge of the woods, while the other featured a fishing boat riding in the easy swell of a blue green sea while gulls circled overhead. We had discovered that pictures of beauty and serenity lent their calmness to troubled children. This little fellow seemed to have a reputation for tempestuousness, so I wanted to waste no time in bringing calm and peace to his world. To help establish a place of his own within his own home, I tacked up a large brown envelope inside the closet for Chris to collect the treasures we would later put in a scrapbook.

Mrs. Jentz called to check in with us. She was thankful to hear that I could hardly contain myself for joy over this great little guy. As her day had drawn to a close, the realization had come to her that she had actually found a home for this difficult-to-place child after one brief visit with us and after scarcely scanning the home study that had been compiled on us. She tried then to call us — repeatedly, in fact. Of course, we were not at home; we were out showing Chris off all over town. Mrs. Jentz said she thought, *They've taken him back to the Children's Home already!* I assured her that we never would. The Lord being our helper, there is no such thing as an unsolvable problem or an impossible situation. Besides, we don't regard children as returnable merchandise.

Our trip to the grocery store was delightful. Chris had never been in a store before! He wasn't doing a whole lot of talking, but he was doing a lot of taking it all in! Regular customers, we introduced him with pride to the employees there. Only a sparse few hours after we had acquired Chris, my concern about his mental abilities was being dispelled. At the grocery store, he pointed out the cats on the cat food boxes that looked like our cats and those that looked like our neighbor cats as well. Using more correct names than I could have on such short acquaintance, Chris called my attention to dog food bags with pictures of dogs like ours. At lunchtime, Chris helped by putting mugs around (each child has his own mug of a different color). By dinnertime, he knew who owned several of them.

All morning I had been wondering what to do about Chris's ankle. It was looking progressively more angry and seemed to trouble him. Early in the afternoon, with the laundry sorted but not started, the groceries yet to be put away, and not the first bit of production accomplished toward the picnic meals, Sherry came in from playing with the children next door and said, "I just stepped on a rusty nail, but I don't have to go to the doctor's, do I?" That ended my indecision about Chris: we all went to the doctor's.

Two hours later we were home again with the knowledge that the soreness on Chris's ankle was caused by a boil, which required an application of salve and four soakings a day in warm water. How I blessed the change in our life-style since Bob had been the only one of that age. Then we would have canceled our plans, stayed at home, and made a production of the treatment. Now we simply added a bucket to our traveling gear and stopped along the way, where gracious restaurant and service station operators filled our bucket and our dear little newcomer spent his soaking time enjoying first glimpses of superhighways, orchards, lakes, bays, lighthouses, and tugboats. Chris had never been on a trip before! They'd done marvels for him at the Children's Home, taking him to the zoo, the circus, and local parks. They had done the very best they could, but to get the most out of life's experiences, a fellow needs a family. A boy who had never been on a picnic, Chris that day alone experienced three, as we breakfasted, lunched, and dinnered picnic fashion.

The weeks following Chris's coming into our family were pure enchantment. Once again we were seeing the whole world as brand new. Chris had never seen a typewriter, had no awareness of air conditioning, never worked a parking meter or visited a library; every kitchen utensil was new to him, as were the soaps, air fresheners, and other goodies that beckoned so temptingly from the linen closet shelves. We scarcely passed the little bathroom without noting the fragrance of a spray tested by curious little fingers. Chris had never been in a school building. He had never gone for a ride in a boat, though once he had been taken swimming — an admirably daring undertaking for a staff with more than a hundred children to protect.

A very few days after Chris came to us, he spied a cement truck. It was en route to a construction job nearby, so we watched it do its work and get its bath. How much more fun for me, I thought, than to be walking the floor and changing the diapers of a newborn. From then on, Chris could and did recognize cement trucks from great distances. The same thing happened with lighthouses, tugboats, anything with which he now had some experience. Ours was a bright little boy, sadly underexperienced until now.

We learned after a few weeks that Chris, too, threw tantrums. I don't recall what it was that triggered the first we were to witness. I recall only my satisfaction, as it developed, in being certain that this was an aspect of child behavior with which I was familiar and could deal effectively. Pride, they say, cometh before the fall.

As I steered our enraged little son to his room, I instructed Chris, as I had Joe before him, to scream and kick to his heart's content; just stay on the bed. He did. But while he was there, he threw everything he could reach as hard as he could throw it. Bang! Crash! Pow! Realizing this was a facet of tantrums that was new to me, I hurried to his room and, duck-

100

ing flying objects, hastily put any valuable, breakable things I could find outside the door. Shouting above his rage, I advised Chris that this was not an acceptable course of action. He yelled louder, glared more viciously, reached further to get his hands on one more thing to throw — at me this time. I ducked the missile, flipped the boy over, and swatted the place the Lord provided, very briefly, for Chris righted himself and started pummeling me. Now I am a very small grown-up, but tough. And he was a very large five-year-old, also very tough, but my child nonetheless, and obviously terribly distressed.

By now the other children had gathered at the door of the bedroom, and Bob and Ann wanted to join the fracas on my side. I appreciated their concern, but a tantrum is only external evidence of severe emotional turmoil, and I didn't want Chris to feel resentments toward his newly acquired brothers and sisters. Besides, I wasn't actually losing. It was about time for Pip to come home from work, and I was feeling the need for his wisdom and stability. My physical effort in the fray was simply to keep Chris from hurting himself or damaging things further. Obviously, neither talk nor spanking had helped. I wrestled him as gently as possible to the soft throw rug on the floor, sustaining only a slightly twisted arm and bent glasses in the process, and sat on him. Because I am small and light and he was a husky, strong youngster, I knew that I was not hurting him. Now he could not hurt himself either. Physically, that was. Rather than have him spend this time resenting me, I decided we should put it to good use. Pinned as he was, I read Chris nursery stories until Pip got home. The older children kept reappearing at the door, and I kept assuring them that Chris and I were doing just fine.

When the father whom Chris reverenced more than the sun and the moon and the stars put together came home, he was of course immediately advised of the scene in the front bedroom. Pip called the other four children and addressed them and Chris in one voice. "This will never happen again!" he declared. "Chris, you will never strike at your mother. You other children, if Chris ever behaves like this again, I want you to deal with him. That is not a request, it is an order. You have no choice." The big kids said that they had wanted to help, and I surely concurred. I had no objection to their helping in the future, now that Chris had been advised what would be the course of action.

The storm over, Chris was a happy youngster again, and we were a wiser family. Full of life, gloriously happy at his happy times, only ever fragilely secure in his belonging, Chris often skated on the thin ice of tumult. You could see the storm clouds gather, and to my relief, yea delight (and constant amazement), Chris could usually be talked out of having a tantrum. I don't mean that we ever gave in to him. Any child would be a tyrant if he got his own way by having a tantrum. With our already insecure children, a policy of giving in to tantrum throwers would have brought chaos. Now, our children knew that they never got their way by having tantrums. Of that they could be certain. But Chris could be reasoned with. He knew tantrum throwing wouldn't bend the rules, and every so often, I could and did take Chris on my lap, assure him of my love for him, and discuss his troubles. Before we were through talking, he would have recovered his usual happy attitude, and all would be well.

Unfortunately, this didn't always work. Sometimes I was not alert to a gathering storm. We learned that once the fury struck, the rage and the throwing would follow. As it set its course, we would steer Chris toward the backyard. Once outside in the fenced yard, he could scream, throw, and kick to his heart's content, damaging nothing. Thirty minutes later — you could almost set the clock by it — his rage spent, the boy would be tired out, and (happily for all of us) his world would be in order again.

As the weeks went on, I became more clever about anticipating circumstances that could trigger a tantrum. Mostly Chris needed to be in the middle of family; any degree of isolation could be devastating. It didn't help things if Chris were hungry either. We learned to serve meals promptly on schedule!

Even a brief chapter about Chris should not close without the story of his adoption day. Because Bob had to work and we couldn't have a full house, and all of the others would have to have been held out of school, we decided not to take anyone but Chris himself. I waited until he had attended the morning session of school. Then, when Chris came home for lunch, I showed him the new outfit we had bought for the occasion and told him the happy particulars of the coming few hours. Chris went to pieces. Words and affection and patience couldn't console him. He manifested every possible insecurity in the next two hours. I really couldn't put a finger on the reason.

We met Pip in a downtown parking lot near to both our attorney's office and the courthouse. I hissed to Pip that Chris was terrified. We walked with him between us, both holding his hand. Pip reiterated the glory of it all, that this was the one last thing to be done to keep us together forever and ever. Soon after

103

arriving at attorney Ben Pine's, we were ushered into his private office, as was usual, so that he could bring us up to date on what to expect in the judge's chamber. Pip continued to hold fast to Chris, trying to reinforce him with his nearness.

Now Ben, a very serious type, wears a constant half frown. The first thing he said was, "Have there been any problems?" Chris turned absolutely white. Had he not been up on his daddy's lap and encircled by his strong and loving arms, I think he would have broken and run. I realized instantly the cause of his terror and broke into such laughter that Chris was at last at his ease. Chris thought they were going to ask if he had been good, and one thing Chris isn't quite a bit of the time is good — enjoyable, every moment, but not particularly good. Once Pip and Ben were also laughing, Chris realized he was off the hook, and it was a good day from then on.

Two little girls were adopted just ahead of us (I reminded Pip that we didn't have a *little* girl). That family came out of the judge's chambers beaming. The judge was wearing his robe, just the way you see them on television. Ben asked Judge McCallister, who had presided at Sherry's adoption proceedings, if he remembered us. He said he did, and he and Pip shook hands. Then we were seated, again with Chris on Pip's knee. The judge had us raise our right hands. Chris raised his as well. The judge, Ben, Pip, and I all had to fight to keep from laughing. The judge was obviously delighted. Needless to say, so were we. The procedure is for the lawyer to ask us questions, such as our name and address, who placed the child with us, when, the date of his birth, if we'd had him to the doctor, and so on. This time, interestingly, I was asked the names of our other children — not their ages or their interests or where we got them, simply their names. The lawyer also directed a question to Pip about the amount of his income. At home later on, Pip and I enjoyed a good laugh. We decided the prerequisites for enlarging our family were simple: Pip had to earn enough money, and I had to be able to remember the children's names!

The moment the questioning was done, the judge granted our petition for adoption, told us we would receive a birth certificate in about forty-five days, and from then on we would get copies from the state board of health. The wonderful strides that have been made in this field in a single generation!

Afterward we went together to the Deluxe Ice Cream Shoppe, where Pip and I drank coffee while we watched Chris eat the biggest tin roof sundae I've ever seen. He'd never seen anything even remotely like it. He stared at it in utter disbelief, then his smile spread out all the way to his ears. He ate the whole thing.

Halloween Haunts and Happiness

I overheard Sherry boasting that she had learned to ride a two-wheeled bicycle in one day, on her first birthday. This startled me, for she *had* learned to ride the day her bike was new — on her *seventh* birthday. Then I realized her seventh was her first birthday with her new family.

Ann was eight on her first birthday, and Joe was five on his. Only two of our children can even remember ever observing a birthday before they became part of this family. It is usual then, in this family, to hear the children discussing what they did, or received, or the kind of cake they had on their first or second birthdays — birthdays celebrated when they were, in point of fact, five to nine years old. First and second birthdays are a lot easier to remember under those circumstances!

Just as they could remember no birthdays before coming to us, Ann and Joe could remember no Halloweens, so it was great fun to choose the pumpkin that could be made into exactly the right jack-o'-lantern and plan the best costume for each child to use in trick-or-treating around the neighborhood, and another for the school party. (Bless the bountiful costume

106

box, stuffed with Bob's costumes from all years past. It held old clothes, cheap jewelry, novelty hats, eye patches, masks, and makeup.) Bunched together, we chilled and thrilled through the spook house. We managed to turn the larger portion of October into a Halloween fiesta.

As that season rolled around the first autumn Sherry was part of the family, we were more than usually eager to make it a happy time. Among the sadnesses she was to relate was her feeling of aloneness the Halloween before, when she, on her own, had to contrive a costume and felt that it was inadequate. From her description of it, though, it had been as proper and gala as many contrived by the children of abundance. Nonetheless, Sherry had felt very much alone and deprived during the Halloween season, and we were bound to make this Halloween a great one. For the most part we succeeded.

On one point only did we fail. We took her to the Haunted House. We tucked her right into the middle of the family group, where the newest child belongs, and all in a bundle inched toward each new "horror," or darted all together to a far side, safely out of the reach of a goblin. We were alternately giggling and squealing, pushing and pulling (Sherry too), when right in the middle of the guided tour, Sherry's squeals of fun suddenly became hysterical screams. The goblin immediately unmasked (bless that man!), while our whole family, as of one voice, tried to assure Sherry that all of the ghosts and goblins were just daddies and mommies. The one who had scared her the most was perhaps the kindest of all, for he tried as hard as we did to reassure her that it was all in fun.

Sherry could not be consoled, and there was nothing to do but for her daddy to pick her up in his arms and carry her swiftly and "safely" through to the exit. While Pip and the older children continued to enjoy spook houses, Sherry and I waited outside for them for the next several years. When, eventually, she felt certain she wanted to enjoy the spooky treat, we waited in line in a cold October rain for thirty minutes. As we reached the door, Sherry turned to me and said, "Mom, I can't." We didn't. We have never attempted to take Chris through the spook house. Sherry's hysteria has taught us that real terror known in early childhood can come surfacing through. Although the terror in Chris's life had come when he was too young to have a conscious remembrance of it, we feared the same reaction.

We had guessed right. On his second Halloween, Chris's teacher called me at home following their party time. "Mrs. Piepenbrink," she began, "a strange thing happened today with Chris, and I thought you ought to know. A few of the mothers dressed up in costumes, and Chris got hysterical with fright. I know that it wasn't pretended; I could tell that he was terrified. I had the mothers unmask and after a while he quieted down, but I know that it was an awful experience for him." I thanked her for calling and told her that I was not surprised. Children who have had cause to be terrified live with fear too close to the surface to play at being frightened. Now, as a family, we relegate Haunted Houses to an optional activity for dating teens and put our emphasis on the amusing, not the spooky, aspects of All Hallows' Eve.

There are lots of them! When he came to us at five, Chris had never heard of Halloween (or pumpkins, for that matter). We attended a fair a full month before Halloween and saw a pumpkin we knew at once would be perfect for our jack-o'-lantern. It had one simple virtue: it was the biggest pumpkin any of us had ever seen. As families are inclined to do all too often, I fear, we relied upon our daddy without consideration for him. None of us, except Pip, thought of the size of the pumpkin in relation to the distance to the car. Ever since we had been a family, we had chosen jack-o'-lanterns-to-be when we were all together so that everyone could have a part in the decision. "You're *sure* this is the one you want?" Pip had asked. "It's still a month till Halloween!" We were! So Pip put the pumpkin on his shoulder and began picking his way through the crowd with the cumbersome burden. By the time he got to the car, many of the people at the fair were assured that this family was going to have a happy Halloween, for Chris ran ahead in his excitement, pointing back to Pip and calling out to all who would notice: "That's my dad! He's got our pumpkin! See that pumpkin? That's ours! That's my dad bringing our pumpkin!"

It did make a grand jack-o'-lantern. After congregating and selecting a pumpkin, each one would draw the face of his choice on a scrap of paper. We would then vote for the face to be used that particular year. Chris's enchantment with the pumpkin never subsided, and his delight in the jack-o'-lantern it became was a joy to behold. In ours as in all too many neighborhoods, pumpkin smashing had become the thing to do. I was protective of this great orange fellow, knowing what he meant to one little boy we had only so recently found. We put him on the doorstep during the early evening hours when the younger children would be about to enjoy his glowing smile and brought him in before the usual time of mischief. Even so, very early in the evening of his second day of life, our great jack-o'-lantern was taken from our doorstep and broken in the street, the mischief-makers never realizing, I'm sure, that it was a little boy's heart that was cruelly broken as well.

We gathered up the pieces, brought them in the house, and were blessedly able to reassemble most of him. A too-large hole where his eye had been we covered with a black, pirate's eye patch. A squashed-apart head we disguised with a great Mexican sombrero. A scarf around his "neck" completed his costume. For the remainder of the season, we kept him safe in the shelter of the house. That great pumpkin enjoyed a lengthy lifetime of surveying a happy family through that one good eye. Very often an enchanted little boy could be observed simply standing, gazing eyeball to eyeball with him as they smiled at each other.

Those who seek the Lord
lack no good thing.
— Psalm 34:10

Family's Fun

Bob had already graduated from high school the happy summer day we drove out to the Children's Home to claim our Chris. We hoped and expected that Bob would begin his college work in our own community, but we could not be certain that he would. There was a good chance that he might have to leave shortly to satisfy his commitment to military service. We were determined, therefore, from the moment Chris came into our lives, to share every hour that we could in the coming weeks so that these two boys could have a great deal to remember should our days together as a total family be few. The result was that at a time when the prime national concern was the demise of family life, ours was blooming.

We ate all of our meals together, even though it meant getting up earlier than need be for most of the family and having dinner later than many families do. If it were impossible for the older children to schedule their working hours (or class hours later, during the school year) away from the dinner hour, we observed special occasions at breakfast time, when we were all always here. Birthday breakfasts are fun. Our first consideration was togetherness of family. For instance, when we were arranging for Ann to fly to visit her grandmother, the flight had not only to be a convenient one for Grandmother to meet, but it also had to have a local departure time that would permit the entire family to see Ann off at the airport.

We geared optional activities around necessary ones so that we might share our comings and goings. On the day Ann needed to be downtown for her music lesson, for example, all of the children and I went to town together rather than send Ann alone on the bus. The rest of us spent the hour visiting the library, then perhaps shopping a bit before we all came home together. That way we knew how Ann's lesson had gone, she knew what stories the other children had read at the library, and we all knew what each one dreamed of buying when he or she had the ready cash.

Among the things we did that special together summer was to take the family, even the dogs, on a business trip. Pip had to be in a city far enough away to necessitate his staying overnight. Rather than miss those precious hours, we decided to go along with him, making a minivacation of it. It turned out to be one of those just-right things you're ever after glad you did. What would have been simply a place for Pip to sleep became the setting for a motel party. All of us enjoyed snacks we had only occasionally. The children (several in each bed), propped up on their pillows, were permitted to watch television as long as they wished! Now, years later, they recall with delight who squiggled the most in the bed and who *really* stayed awake the very longest. To think how easily we could have missed acquiring that rich storehouse of wonderful memories had we not had a fetish for family!

Most evenings we took a walk, all together, around our neighborhood or browsed the stores of the nearby shopping center. The children would have running races ahead and back again to us (two of them are outstanding runners in competition today). Sometimes we would take a basketball or a big plastic bat and ball and have a family ball game in the school yard. There are so very many things for families to do together that cost little or nothing. Some of our favorites were the shopping malls, where there is almost always a free exhibit or demonstration, and household auctions, where the children grew in knowledge of furnishings and gadgets unlike those in our own home. We visited county and small-town fairs in nearby communities and had wonderful times picking our own apples and eating them. The highlight of many a week was the drive-through car wash. Try that with an underexperienced child and a curious pup; chalk the cost up to entertainment.

Family outings were planned around the special interests of family members. The very first trip Chris ever took was a long day's outing to a nearby state so that Bob could be in a war-games tournament. (Using tin soldiers, players reenact actual historic battles. Weather reports, rolls of the dice, and the expertise of the players determine the outcome.) We took Bob and two of his friends, enjoying their companionship on the way, hearing of their hopes and plans for the day. While the boys had their match, we picnicked and went sightseeing. We picked them up at the finish of the match, just in time to hear their blow-by-blow accounts of the action. On those occasions when the band was in a contest and Ann rode with her fellow band members on a school bus, the rest of the family would travel to the contest to share the day and the memory, as we did when Joe would run cross-country or track. During the school year, our evenings out very

113

frequently were and are each other's school concerts, carnivals, and athletic events. An event for one is an occasion for all. If a member of our family is involved, you can depend on a built-in cheering section.

By the time Bob was serving his stint on active duty with the Air National Guard, we were so geared to doing and being together that it was lonely for any of us to be separated even briefly. We all wrote to him so often that it was almost embarrassing. His first mail call brought him seventeen pieces of mail! At the conclusion of his training, when we all — including Bob's girl and Brute — drove across several states to visit him in camp, it was pretty obvious that there wasn't a guy there who wouldn't have been glad to have just such a family descend upon him. Surely Bob deserved to have home brought to him while he was away from home. After all, the large, happy family that then was his might never have been had he not so willingly shared his home, his parents, and his siblings.

Quite by accident in some instances, by courtesy of Mother Necessity in others, our life-style became more relaxed and pleasant. Chris came to us with a sore ankle the day we planned on having a picnic. We simply bagged up the picnic fixings and took them along. Instead of making sandwiches in a hot kitchen, we made some of them under a tall pine tree near a sparkling lake, others by a babbling brook near a roadside rest. Later we decided to take no picnic supplies, buying them instead from stores near our destination. We always found something to enjoy in unfamiliar stores along the way. Sometimes it would be fruit from a roadside stand, or perhaps some goodies from a bake sale. We encountered interesting people as well as different foods. Best of all, the mother of the family wasn't all tired out from preparing lunches!

Because there were so many of us and so many things we wanted to do, we were forced to find a more efficient routine. Just as soon as each child was old enough, that child was taught to do whatever tasks his or her age, sense of responsibility, intelligence, and coordination allowed — from dusting to driving. We happily discovered that during the summer months, when youngsters were free from the demands of school, they could assume some of the jobs I took care of during the school year. With everyone doing a part, we could get the work done and still have a day or two free each week for outings or special activities. I was surprised to discover that workdays, when no play or social commitments were allowed, were often the happiest days of the week. Even young children find satisfaction in being useful, we observed.

What was good for the goslings was good for the goose. I was forever forgetting to take the hamburger from the freezer or to set the Jello. I discovered it saved far more time to spend a little of it writing a meal plan, which I taped inside the kitchen cabinet. You can imagine my pleasure one day when I arrived home in a tizzy minutes before Pip to discover that the older children had followed the meal plan and had dinner ready and waiting.

The father of our family likes to do things spontaneously. It is the flip side of his personality, for his responsibilities are met always with the most stringent regularity after careful planning. This yen to pick up in the middle of a Sunday afternoon and go swimming or to decide at dinnertime that if we hurry, we can make a movie that begins in forty-five minutes keeps life from ever getting dull. It also has necessitated a family policy of involving ourselves in play on weekends and holidays with family members only. After an incident of conflict, when some of us wanted to go and others were playing with neighbor children and wanted to stay, we made it a rule that whenever Pip was home, our commitments would be only with each other, keeping us entirely flexible. The result was the happy opening of another door.

Now, it is a regrettable fact that our children fight with each other just as brothers and sisters everywhere do. They are absolutely usual in their relationships with each other, even though I sometimes think they shouldn't be. It strikes me that we are more blessed than a conventional family in the very fact of having found each other. The children think so too — till the adjustment period is over. Then, as surely as honeymoons do end, the "fun" begins. The thing we learned from insisting on playtime involving children in our family only, was that during these times they do not fight. When they don't have the option of bringing in a neighbor child or trading a brother for a friend, they will play for hours on end without a bit of friction or unpleasantness. This enforced togetherness — or prohibited separateness — results in greater understanding and appreciation of each other. After these playtimes, we are apt to hear: "That G.I. Joe of Chris's used to be Joe's, and it's so old it's coming apart and isn't much fun for him. Could we get him a new one for his birthday?" Or: "I'm going to make a new dress for Eve's doll. She'll like that. Her doll doesn't have a formal."

The older children discovered that the younger ones came to us not really knowing how to play. Even apart from those times when family togetherness was required, they arranged their own busy routines to play both ball and board games with the little ones to help them develop a willingness for taking turns and a spirit of fair play. We can only guess at the number of problems we haven't had in other areas of our children's lives because their siblings cared that much.

We're not one of those families who don't watch television. We enjoy TV, too, and this too we share. We *do* know where the off button is and how to use it. Hardly a day goes by, however, when we don't have the television on for a little while. As a dating couple Pip and I loved to go to the movies. And while we really regret the near demise of good movies, we find it a wonderful convenience to have enjoyable stories presented in the comfort of our living room. Family members have learned to take turns, when there is a time conflict, in watching favorite shows. The exception to the rule is Father's football. As provider for us all, the few hours he has for television viewing are never contested; the children become intelligent spectators years ahead of themselves.

For a time, we resisted the temptation to purchase a second set, feeling it would cost us togetherness. We ultimately succumbed, but not until the game room became the place where the oldest children entertained their friends and we thought it would be fun for them. On very special occasions we permit its use by the younger children, but it must be a special set of circumstances indeed.

There have been times, certainly, when one or several of us would rather have abstained from family participation, perhaps for good reasons. But after only a little while of obligatory togetherness, we have learned a lot about and from each other. A little learning grew gradually into a lot of loving appreciation for each other and loving concern for the other's weaknesses. After that, a great many wonderful fringe benefits have come rolling in.

117

*Now faith is
the assurance of things hoped for,
the conviction of things not seen.*
— Hebrews 11:1

Eventually Eve

We knew it was time that they would have Eve for us.
We had had a Lay Witness Mission at our church that
weekend, and as a result of our praying together about
our next child, we felt that she would be ready for us.
On Monday Pip went into the office of the woman
now heading our adoption division and said he
thought she would be wanting to talk with him.

"Why, Mr. Piepenbrink," she responded in surprise, "I do. But how did you know? Who called you?
I hadn't told anyone to get in touch with you."

"Oh, no one had," Pip assured her, "but we've
been praying about it. I knew there would be word."

There was. There had been a single stumbling
block in the way, Mrs. Byrd told Pip, but it had been
removed that very weekend. Now, if we were willing,
the necessary paperwork could begin.

This was the first time we had had to specify that
we were only willing to take a girl, for the newcomer
would have to share a room with Sherry. Eve was just
a year younger than Chris. Pip learned that morning
that she had been badly burned and was still receiving
treatments. As a three-year-old, she had stood on an
oven door while trying to cook herself something to

118

eat, and her clothing had caught fire. Given the best of care in a Shriners' Burns Institute, she made a good recovery, only to find, after her return from the hospital, that she had no homelife to come back to. She bounced, therefore, from being queen of the ball at the hospital to being one of the crowd at the Children's Home. As a result, Eve thought of hospitals as happy places.

We had to wait several weeks before they brought Eve to us. During that time we were very restless as a family. One afternoon I told a friend that I would not be going out and would not call her again until the next day because I was sure they were going to contact us about Eve. They did. They said her caseworker would be bringing her on Friday and she could stay until Sunday evening. Then later — should we still be so inclined — she could be ours for keeps. Of course, we wanted her to come. We *knew* we wanted to keep her. There had been no question of that since the moment we heard of her. We did not want a visit arrangement; we wanted her to stay. Forever and ever.

We contested this over the next few days until the welfare department's adoption division played its trump card. They would have her visit with some other family over this weekend. Then, when she was ready for placement, she could come to us to stay. We liked that proposal even less. We had to have her, and we had to have her then; we'd just have to take our chances on keeping her.

So, on another wintry Friday evening, another little girl came to us, for the weekend, lugging a brown paper bag full of clothes and some books and playthings. Whatever I expected — and I had no real preconceived notion — she was not it. Eve was no bigger than a minute. We had been told that she was tiny. She wore thick-lensed, horn-rimmed glasses, and her thick, straight hair completely covered her forehead in bangs and, in its fullness, much of the rest of her face. The only part of her face showing was scarred from her burns. Recalling Sherry's belligerence, and not really being able to see much of Eve's expression, I sat down on the couch — but not too close. I succeeded in keeping my distance for only a few minutes. Her nearness and her dearness were too much for me. I soon scooped Eve up onto my lap, where she stayed.

All our experience was useless under these circumstances. We wanted to keep this child forever and ever, we thought she wanted to stay, yet we all had to endure a visit arrangement. Between the time we had learned that Chris was awaiting adoption and this time, our county's welfare division had been reorganized and an adoption unit established. The fine woman who headed this unit knew of every child in the county who was available for adoption and of every approved adoptive home. What a giant step in the right direction! Yet we had a difference of opinion as to the best way to place a child in a home. Always before, we had insisted that our child was to be ours from the first moment we met. Looks, personality, behavior — these had nothing to do with it. We felt a visit added to the trauma from which these children already suffered. We had tried insisting that Eve come to stay, but they had outmaneuvered us. Now that we had this silent wisp of humanity in our home, we pleaded again for permission to keep her. The caseworker who brought her was powerless. Though she pretty much agreed with her boss that a visit first was a good arrangement, we were certain she would have yielded to our pressure if she'd had the option.

Now we were hamstrung. We knew the new children needed to be kept busy, and this one did if ever one did, uncertain as she was of her status. We crammed more activity into that one weekend than we would have into a usual month's worth of weekends. When we weren't visiting or shopping, we went to ball games, movies, and to church, of course. Eve hadn't come with a thing to wear to church that was of the standard the rest of us owned. The clothing she wore, like the clothing she brought, was out of style: the dresses a little too long, the pants a little too short. The inadequacy of her wardrobe left me a little mystified, especially after having received Chris from the very same institution fully and adequately equipped with all the fine clothes he could wear, not to mention a supply of toys and books he enjoyed. Eve surely looked the role of a poor little waif. We corrected that by the next afternoon. By Sunday we corrected the other "error."

From early Saturday morning on, Pip was on the phone almost hourly to one person or another, trying to gain permission to keep Eve. He even tried to go "over the head" of our adoption unit officer. There was no string he would not pull, for we were certain that returning Eve to the Children's Home, however briefly, would add to her mountain of insecurities in a way that might take months or years to correct. The closest we came to winning the battle was to obtain an absolute promise that Eve would be returned to us to stay on Tuesday.

With that assurance, Pip took Eve to the bedroom she was to share with Sherry and told her that this was her room, forever and ever. That bottom bunk she had slept in last night was her bed, the middle drawer and half of the bottom one were hers, this half of the closet was hers. This new dress and her new Sunday shoes were hers. We explained that we would have to take her back to the Children's Home — *as a visitor* — for two nights while they typed up the proper papers. Then, on Tuesday, she would be back in this, her home with us, her forever-and-ever family.

My, but we were a sad carful as we drove out to leave our precious new one for her final "visit" at the Children's Home. But we were a happy, happy family when she was returned bright and early on Tuesday morning. This time she came beautifully dressed, equipped with an abundant wardrobe, including many brand-new things, and so many toys, dolls, games, and stuffed animals that the caseworker was hard put to fit them in her little car. It occurred to me then that the "pitiful waif" appearance Eve achieved on her weekend visit was a subtle trick of a caring housemother. Surely this youngster needed a home and family, so she had been sent out *looking* as though she needed a home and family!

On the evening of the day Eve came to us, she said: "This is really a happy day. I didn't have to go to school *all day!*"

Ask, and you will receive,
that your joy may be full.
— John 16:24

Good Gifts Garnished

Eve was a bonus. We had suspected that she would be since before we applied for her. We had never relented in our search for Ann and Joe because we wanted a family of three children and, most especially, because we did not want Bob to have to go through life without the companionship of a brother and sister. We were fully satisfied with our family after their coming. It was only after our encounter with little Jody made us aware that there were waiting children that we considered adding to our family.

We were concerned about whether we could afford another child. We prayed about it, knowing that if it were God's will for our lives, He would make it clear to us. We were enjoying financial gains in every facet of our lives just then; so, having received such encouragement, we never relented until Sherry was a part of our family. We believed that Sherry was a special gift God gave us because we were trying to help Him fulfill His purpose in the world. We *could*, all of us agreed, take one more. Now, with our wealth of experience, we thought we were ready for a child who might find the adjustment to family living too great to make in some other family.

In reviewing the paperwork, Chris seemed to fit that description. Yet we knew he was a very special treasure from the moment we laid eyes on him. By the time we applied for Eve, we had pretty well quit kidding ourselves: every child is a very special treasure. And every time we made an all-out effort to do something special to serve God, He turned it around so that we were the ones who were blessed.

Eve had been our little girl for scarcely a week when she bounded past us one evening on her way to the playroom with the other children, giggling happily as she went. Pip spoke his thoughts as well as my own: "We needed her!" Truly, we did.

She needed us, too; everyone needs a forever-and-ever family. In a matter of days, Eve had learned how to say and spell her new name, and she would defy the entire staff of the hospital whenever they attempted to call her by her former name. She learned all there was to learn about all of her aunts and uncles and cousins, took them to her heart before ever she could meet them, wrote to them, and claimed them as well as each of us for her very own. Like Ann before her, she was a marvel with our pets, of which there were now half a dozen. At a time when sheer numbers and the accompanying increase in the commotion level occasionally meant a late meal for people and animals alike, the pets were more than satisfied with the arrangement because of the loving interest our newest newcomer showed in each of them.

When we volunteered to have Eve's end-of-the-year class picnic in our backyard, her teacher and I got our signals crossed as to which date was the "last week of the school year." Notes had been sent out reminding students about the picnic to be held at our house the next day — a full seven days ahead of the time I had anticipated it! Once I recovered my breath and my wit, it was really no problem. Ann drove over to the grocery store for cake and Kool-Aid mixes (things we had agreed to supply), while Sherry quickly mopped the kitchen floor, getting that chore out of the way ahead of the more pleasurable task of baking the cakes. Ann prepared the Kool-Aid and stored it in the refrigerator, Joe and Bob made sure the backyard was company clean, and the little children gave special emphasis to the daily chores of dusting and vacuuming. It was my intention that Eve's teacher would never know our calendar had worn a different date than hers.

Late that night, however, she realized what had happened and called to express her concern. When I told her we were ready, waiting, and eager, she responded, "I thank you for your organization!" While I had searched and yearned and waited for that Good Gift to walk in by the front door, her choice of words compelled me to agree that it had sneaked in by the back. All unawares had I been of its form and presence!

The End Becomes the Beginning

If you would approach your later middle years without a concern for your health, with no serious financial worries, with a sense of purpose about each hour and every day, adopt a child awaiting a home. Or adopt several. Nothing special is required. The adoption picture has changed. You don't have to be young or in particularly good health. You may have natural ("biological") children and be able to have more. Certainly you don't have to be well heeled or own your own home.

You do have to be willing to disclose the amount of your income, the size of your bank account (if you boast one), and the heights and depths of your plans and dreams to interviewing social workers. Beyond this, you must show a dog-with-his-bone persistence about finding *your* child (or children), and NOW! Caseworkers can and do measure your ability and willingness to deal with the child's problems and your problems with that child by the tenacity you demonstrate in seeking your child.

Although we often thought we were in deep water during the years you have just read about, we were really only building a foundation for what lay ahead.

The *Forever Family* story, as we think of our own lives, is but an introduction, a time of preparation. The present time is one of both happy reflection and minute-to-minute challenge.

Bob and Ann are grown now and married to people as wondrously special as they are themselves. All of them are exemplary citizens, supportive of Pip and me in every way as we struggle to rear the "impossible" children who are their younger brothers and sisters today. Joe ultimately learned to take orders well enough to qualify himself to give them. He is a sergeant in the United States Army and proudly plans to make the military his career. Sherry, as pretty and delightful as she has always been, continues living here at home while she studies nursing. Needless to say, Pip and I are delighted with the arrangement.

When Sherry came to us, she was the youngest of our foursome. Today she is oldest of the six children still at home. The story of those transition years is a book unto itself — one that I'm busy writing. In it, I tell of Chris and Eve, growing gradually into congenial, hardworking high-school students, and how Pip and I gathered up the courage to take on children who were more terribly neglected and abused, and ever more challenging. There is the explosive, towheaded Andy; the dark, almost dismal David, who very appropriately has dubbed himself Heap Big Thundercloud; and, finally (well, most recently), Lee, our current Kindergarten Kid, a whirling dervish of smiling femininity with a flair for mischievousness that appalls even us. The story to come details even greater challenges, which I hope to share with you. Pip and I frankly hope that our story will encourage readers to consider providing "forever families" for other children who, at this moment, are still waiting.

Be prepared, if you do, to discover that the world is full of wonderful people.

Our problem with Sherry's need for a reading readiness class in a school that did not offer it was solved by a wonderful teacher who volunteered to keep this little newcomer in a seat near her desk in a first-grade classroom, tutoring her as needed. She also arranged to have her again the following year so that she might be sure this youngster had the foundation she needed.

The holes in Chris's learning were plugged in large part by a neighbor who tutored Chris at no charge for two years. We're grateful, too, to the young dentist who, seeing the terror in a little boy who had known too much of suffering, succeeded in examining his teeth while kneeling on the floor beside him and offering small talk.

There has never been a time, though our wit and wisdom seemed severely challenged on a variety of occasions, when an answer has not come through either a new insight or a kind person. God just does not lead us out on a limb and allow it to be sawed off behind us. That's an observation from people who have climbed out on a lot of limbs in recent years and discovered that many of them turn out to be bridges.